THE DIVINE WARRIOR

LESSONS FROM THE LIFE OF LORD HANUMAN

MUKESH BHARTI

Made with ♥ on the Notion Press Platform
www.notionpress.com

This book is lovingly dedicated to the boundless spirit of devotion, courage, and humility that Lord Hanuman represents.

To those who seek strength in moments of doubt,
To those who find solace in unwavering faith,
To those who strive to embody loyalty, selflessness, and perseverance in their daily lives—
this work is for you.

May the divine teachings of Lord Hanuman inspire you to face life's challenges with valor, overcome obstacles with grace, and remain steadfast in the pursuit of truth and purpose.

To the eternal seeker within all of us,
this book is a humble offering.

Contents

Foreword

In every era and culture, certain figures transcend the boundaries of time to become symbols of ideals that inspire humanity. Lord Hanuman is one such figure—a divine embodiment of strength, humility, and devotion. His stories, as recounted in the ancient Indian epic Ramayana and numerous other texts, continue to guide millions around the world, offering profound lessons that are just as relevant today as they were thousands of years ago.

The Divine Warrior: Lessons from the Life of Lord Hanuman is not merely a collection of stories; it is a roadmap for living a life of purpose, resilience, and service. Through this book, the reader is invited to delve deep into Hanuman's life, exploring his extraordinary qualities, his unyielding devotion to Lord Rama, and his unparalleled ability to overcome challenges with courage and wisdom.

What sets this book apart is its ability to draw parallels between Hanuman's divine virtues and the challenges we face in our modern world. The author masterfully connects ancient wisdom with contemporary life, making this book a beacon for those seeking inspiration, motivation, and personal growth.

As you turn the pages of this work, you will discover not only the heroic deeds of a celestial warrior but also the profound lessons that these deeds convey. Hanuman's humility teaches us to stay grounded in the face of success. His loyalty reminds us of the value of unwavering commitment. His strength, both physical and moral, inspires us to face life's trials with determination and grace.

This book is a treasure trove of timeless teachings that have the power to transform lives. It will inspire readers to embrace Hanuman's qualities, apply his wisdom to their own challenges, and ultimately, embark on a journey toward self-discovery and fulfillment.

May this work bring you closer to the divine essence of Lord Hanuman and help you realize the extraordinary potential within yourself.

Preface

"The Divine Warrior: Lessons from the Life of Lord Hanuman" is a journey into the heart and soul of one of the most revered figures in Hindu mythology. Lord Hanuman, the embodiment of devotion, strength, humility, and wisdom, is not just a character in an ancient epic but a living symbol of the virtues that humanity strives to achieve. His story, as told through the Ramayana and other sacred texts, is more than just a tale of heroism and divine intervention; it is a blueprint for living a life of purpose, integrity, and spiritual fulfillment.

This book seeks to explore the many facets of Hanuman's personality, his actions, and the profound lessons that can be drawn from his life. Hanuman's journey is one of extraordinary feats and divine grace, but it is also a journey that reflects the struggles, challenges, and triumphs that we all experience in our own lives. By delving deep into the various episodes of Hanuman's life—his miraculous birth, his unwavering devotion to Lord Rama, his incredible strength and wisdom, and his ultimate realization of his divine purpose—we can uncover timeless teachings that are as relevant today as they were thousands of years ago.

In writing **"The Divine Warrior,"** my goal is to bridge the ancient wisdom of Hanuman's life with the contemporary challenges we face in the modern world. Each chapter not only recounts the legendary stories of Hanuman but also offers an analysis of the moral and spiritual lessons embedded within these narratives. These lessons are not just for those who follow the Hindu faith; they are universal principles that can guide anyone on the path to personal and spiritual growth.

Hanuman's life is a testament to the power of devotion—devotion not only to a higher power but also to the values and principles that define our humanity. His strength is not just physical but moral and spiritual, teaching us that true power comes from within. His humility is a reminder that greatness is not measured by achievements alone but by the integrity and compassion with which we live our lives. And his wisdom, grounded in love and righteousness, shows us the way to navigate the complexities of life with grace and discernment.

As you embark on this journey through the life of Lord Hanuman, I invite you to reflect on the lessons that resonate with you, to consider how Hanuman's example can inspire you in your own life, and to embrace the virtues that Hanuman so beautifully embodies. Whether you are seeking spiritual insight, personal empowerment, or simply a deeper understanding of one of Hinduism's most beloved figures, I hope that this book will offer you the guidance and inspiration you seek.

May the divine warrior, Lord Hanuman, guide you on your path, and may his life be a beacon of strength, wisdom, and devotion in your own journey.

Acknowledgements

Writing "**The Divine Warrior: Lessons from the Life of Lord Hanuman**" has been a deeply fulfilling journey, and I am grateful to many individuals whose support and encouragement have made this book possible. This project would not have come to fruition without the contributions, insights, and inspiration of several key people and sources.

First and foremost, I extend my heartfelt thanks to my family and friends for their unwavering support and encouragement throughout the writing process. Your belief in this project provided the motivation and strength needed to see it through. To my partner, whose patience and understanding have been a constant source of comfort, thank you for being my rock and sounding board.

I am deeply indebted to the scholars, researchers, and authors whose works have provided valuable insights and context for this book. The study of Lord Hanuman's life and teachings is enriched by the contributions of many esteemed writers and historians. Their extensive research and scholarly work have been instrumental in shaping the narratives and analyses presented in this book.

Special thanks go to my mentors and advisors, who offered guidance and wisdom as I delved into the profound teachings of Lord Hanuman. Your expertise and encouragement have greatly influenced my understanding and interpretation of these timeless lessons.

I also want to acknowledge the various communities and organizations dedicated to the study and preservation of Hindu mythology and spiritual traditions. Your commitment to sharing and sustaining these ancient teachings has provided a wealth of resources and inspiration. The temples, cultural institutions, and online platforms that celebrate and educate about Lord Hanuman have been invaluable in bringing this project to life.

To the readers and devotees who have shared their personal stories and experiences with Hanuman, your insights have added depth and richness to this book. Your enthusiasm and reverence for Lord Hanuman have been a continuous source of inspiration.

In writing this book, I have endeavored to honor the legacy of Lord Hanuman and to share his profound teachings with a wider audience. May this work serve as a source of inspiration and guidance, and may it contribute to the ongoing appreciation and understanding of the divine warrior's enduring wisdom.

With deepest gratitude and respect,

Mukesh Bharti

Prologue

In the vast tapestry of Indian mythology, few characters resonate as profoundly across generations as Lord Hanuman. He is the epitome of devotion, a symbol of strength, and an eternal inspiration for humanity. To know Hanuman is to understand the essence of unwavering faith, selfless service, and unshakable resolve.

This book, The Divine Warrior: Lessons from the Life of Lord Hanuman, is an invitation to journey into the life of this extraordinary figure—not merely as a mythological hero, but as a guide and mentor for navigating the complexities of our modern lives. Through his tales of valor, wisdom, and humility, Hanuman speaks to our innermost challenges, encouraging us to rise above adversity with the same courage and grace that he embodied.

The story of Hanuman is one of overcoming insurmountable odds. From leaping across oceans to carrying mountains, his feats of strength and determination are legendary. But beneath these grand exploits lies an equally powerful narrative of inner strength, moral clarity, and boundless humility. Hanuman teaches us that true power is not measured by what we conquer outwardly but by how we conquer ourselves.

As we face a world filled with uncertainty, stress, and distraction, Hanuman's lessons are more relevant than ever. He reminds us of the importance of staying grounded in faith, of dedicating ourselves to a higher purpose, and of using our abilities for the benefit of others. His life is a testament to the potential within all of us to rise above the ordinary and achieve the extraordinary.

This book does not merely recount Hanuman's stories; it seeks to extract the deeper lessons hidden within them. It bridges the gap between ancient wisdom and contemporary application, showing how the values and virtues of Hanuman can illuminate our paths today. Whether you are seeking guidance, motivation, or simply a connection to something greater, this book is a humble offering to inspire and uplift.

As you turn the pages of this book, may you discover the boundless strength of Hanuman within yourself. May his devotion ignite your faith, his courage bolster your resolve, and his humility remind you of the beauty of selfless service. The journey of Hanuman is not just his story—it is a reflection of the divine potential within us all.

Welcome to the timeless teachings of Lord Hanuman. May his blessings guide you always.

CHAPTER I

Introduction

The Timeless Relevance of Lord Hanuman

Understanding the Divine Warrior: Hanuman's Role in Ancient Wisdom and Modern Life

In the vast and intricate tapestry of Hindu mythology, few figures stand as tall and as revered as Lord Hanuman. Known as the monkey god, Hanuman occupies a unique place in the hearts of millions, not just in India, but across the globe. His stories, rooted in ancient scriptures like the Ramayana, the Mahabharata, and various Puranas, are much more than tales of divine intervention and miraculous feats. They offer profound lessons on devotion, courage, humility, and wisdom, which resonate deeply even in the contemporary world.

Lord Hanuman is a multifaceted deity, embodying qualities that are both divine and deeply human. To his devotees, he is the embodiment of unwavering devotion, the ultimate servant of Lord Rama, and a paragon of strength and courage. However, beyond his physical prowess and legendary feats, Hanuman's story is also one of spiritual depth and inner transformation. His journey from a mischievous and curious child to a wise and powerful servant of Rama symbolizes the potential for growth and self-realization inherent in every human being.

The significance of Hanuman in Hindu culture cannot be overstated. He is worshipped not just as a god, but as an ideal. The Hanuman Chalisa, a 40-verse hymn dedicated to him, is one of the most recited prayers in the Hindu tradition, believed to offer protection, strength, and blessings. Temples dedicated to Hanuman are found in every corner of India, where his image, usually depicted with a mace in one hand and a mountain in the other, serves as a symbol of devotion, power, and the triumph of good over evil.

But who is Hanuman, really? How did he come to be revered as one of the most powerful deities in Hinduism? What makes his story so compelling that it has been told and retold across generations, transcending time, geography, and cultural boundaries? And most importantly, what can we learn from his life that can help us navigate the challenges of our own?

To answer these questions, we must delve deep into the life and character of Hanuman, exploring not just the major events of his life as depicted in the Ramayana and other scriptures, but also the underlying qualities that make him a source of inspiration and guidance.

The Divine Origins of Hanuman

Hanuman's story begins with a unique confluence of divine will and cosmic events. He is born to Anjana, a celestial nymph cursed to live on earth as a monkey, and Kesari, a powerful vanara (monkey) king. However, Hanuman's true parentage is far more complex. He is also considered the son of Vayu, the wind god, who plays a crucial role in his birth. According to the legend, Anjana was performing intense penance to be freed from her curse, and as a result of her devotion, Vayu infused divine energy into her, leading to the birth of Hanuman. This divine parentage endowed Hanuman with supernatural abilities—strength, speed, agility, and the ability to fly.

From the very beginning, Hanuman's life was marked by his divine heritage. As a child, he was extraordinarily powerful and possessed a boundless curiosity that often got him into trouble. The most famous of his childhood exploits is his attempt to eat the sun, mistaking it for a ripe fruit. As the story goes, the infant Hanuman leapt into the sky and chased the sun, causing chaos in the heavens. It was only after the gods intervened that he was stopped, and his powers were temporarily suppressed by a curse that made him forget his divine abilities. This curse, however, was not just a punishment; it was also a way to ensure that Hanuman's powers would only be revealed when truly needed, thereby teaching him humility and the importance of self-control.

This early episode in Hanuman's life is rich with symbolic meaning. The image of a young monkey leaping towards the sun is not just an amusing anecdote; it represents the boundless potential and aspirations of the human spirit. Hanuman's leap symbolizes the innate drive within all of us to reach for the impossible, to seek out the divine, and to transcend our earthly limitations. However, his subsequent fall and the temporary suppression of his powers also serve as a reminder that true strength lies not in unchecked ambition, but in humility, discipline, and the ability to recognize one's place in the larger cosmic order.

The Meeting with Rama: The Birth of Devotion

The turning point in Hanuman's life, and perhaps the most significant moment in the entire Ramayana, is his meeting with Lord Rama. This encounter is not just a meeting between two divine beings; it is the beginning of a relationship that would define Hanuman's existence and elevate him to the status of the greatest devotee in Hindu tradition.

Rama, the prince of Ayodhya, is an incarnation of Vishnu, the preserver of the universe. His story, as told in the Ramayana, is one of dharma (righteousness), duty, and sacrifice. When Hanuman first meets Rama, he is serving Sugriva, the exiled king of the vanaras, who is seeking help to reclaim his throne from his brother, Vali. Hanuman is sent to find out who Rama and his brother Lakshmana are, as they wander through the forest in search of Sita, Rama's wife, who has been abducted by the demon king Ravana.

Disguised as a brahmin, Hanuman approaches Rama and Lakshmana, but as soon as he meets Rama, something profound happens. Hanuman instantly recognizes Rama as his lord and master, and from that moment on, his life is dedicated to serving Rama. This meeting is described with great emotion in the Ramayana, highlighting the deep spiritual connection between the two. For Hanuman, this is not just the beginning of a lifelong service; it is the moment of his spiritual awakening, where his true purpose in life is revealed.

Hanuman's devotion to Rama is the cornerstone of his character. Unlike other gods and heroes in Hindu mythology, Hanuman's greatness does not lie in his powers or his achievements, but in his unwavering loyalty and devotion to Rama. He sees himself not as a god, but as a servant, and it is this humility that makes him so beloved. Hanuman's devotion is not motivated by desire for reward or recognition; it is pure, selfless, and unconditional. He serves Rama not because he seeks to gain anything, but because it is his dharma, his sacred duty.

In this sense, Hanuman's devotion serves as a powerful lesson for all of us. In a world where success is often measured by wealth, power, and status, Hanuman teaches us the value of selfless service and the importance of dedicating ourselves to a higher cause. His life shows us that true fulfillment comes not from seeking to elevate ourselves, but from humbling ourselves in the service of others. This is a lesson that is particularly relevant in today's fast-paced, competitive world, where the pressure to succeed can often lead to stress, burnout, and a sense of emptiness. By following Hanuman's example, we can find a deeper sense of purpose and meaning in our lives.

The Power of Humility and Strength

One of the most striking aspects of Hanuman's character is the balance between his immense strength and his deep humility. In the Ramayana, Hanuman performs incredible feats of strength and courage. He leaps across the ocean to Lanka, defeats powerful demons, lifts mountains, and even challenges the mighty Ravana. Yet, despite all these accomplishments, Hanuman never once seeks to glorify himself. Instead, he attributes all his successes to Rama and remains humble and unassuming throughout.

This humility is not just a personality trait; it is a reflection of Hanuman's spiritual wisdom. He understands that his powers are not his own, but gifts from the divine, to be used in the service of dharma. This is why, despite being one of the most powerful beings in the universe, Hanuman always sees himself as a mere servant of Rama. His humility is what makes him truly great, for it allows him to remain focused on his duty without being distracted by ego or pride.

The balance between strength and humility is a key lesson that Hanuman offers us. In our own lives, we often face the challenge of balancing our personal ambitions and desires with the need to remain grounded and humble. Hanuman's example shows us that true strength is not about dominating others or asserting our superiority, but about serving others and using our abilities for the greater good. By cultivating humility, we can avoid the pitfalls of ego and pride, and remain focused on what truly matters.

Overcoming Impossible Odds: The Leap to Lanka

One of the most famous episodes in the Ramayana is Hanuman's leap to Lanka in search of Sita. This mission is a turning point in the war against Ravana, and it is here that Hanuman truly shines as a hero. The task before him is daunting: to cross the vast ocean that separates India from Lanka, find Sita, and bring back information to Rama. The challenges are immense, but Hanuman faces them with unwavering determination and courage.

As Hanuman prepares to leap across the ocean, he faces several obstacles. First, he must overcome the doubts and fears of those around him. The other vanaras are unsure if Hanuman can make the leap, and even Hanuman himself is momentarily unsure of his abilities. However, with the encouragement of Jambavan, the wise bear, Hanuman remembers his divine powers and resolves to take on the challenge.

As he soars through the sky, Hanuman encounters several other obstacles, including the demoness Surasa, who tries to swallow him, and the mountain Mainaka, which offers him rest. But Hanuman overcomes each of these challenges with a combination of strength, wisdom, and determination. He does not allow fear or doubt to hold him back, nor does he succumb to the temptation of rest. Instead, he remains focused on his mission and presses forward with unwavering resolve.

This episode is rich with symbolic meaning and offers valuable lessons for all of us. Hanuman's leap to Lanka represents the courage and determination required to overcome life's challenges. In our own lives, we often face obstacles that seem insurmountable—whether it is a difficult job, a personal crisis, or a daunting goal. Hanuman's example teaches us that with faith in ourselves and our abilities, and with the determination to press forward, we can overcome even the most difficult challenges.

Moreover, Hanuman's journey to Lanka also teaches us the importance of focus and perseverance. In a world full of distractions, it is easy to lose sight of our goals and become discouraged. But Hanuman's unwavering focus on his mission shows us that by staying true to our purpose and remaining committed to our goals, we can achieve success, no matter how difficult the path may be.

Righteous Anger: The Burning of Lanka

After finding Sita in Ravana's palace and delivering Rama's message to her, Hanuman is captured by Ravana's forces. Despite being chained and brought before Ravana, Hanuman remains calm and composed. He uses the opportunity to try and reason with Ravana, urging him to return Sita to Rama and avoid the destruction of his kingdom. However, Ravana, blinded by pride and arrogance, refuses to listen and orders that Hanuman's tail be set on fire.

In response, Hanuman uses his divine powers to escape his captors and, with his tail ablaze, leaps from building to building, setting Lanka on fire. The burning of Lanka is one of the most dramatic and powerful scenes in the Ramayana, symbolizing the destruction of evil and the power of righteous anger.

However, it is important to understand that Hanuman's anger is not the uncontrolled rage of a vengeful being. It is a righteous anger, directed at the forces of evil and injustice. Hanuman's actions are motivated not by a desire for revenge, but by a sense of duty and justice. He knows that the destruction of Lanka is necessary to weaken Ravana's forces and pave the way for Rama's victory.

This episode teaches us an important lesson about the nature of anger. In our own lives, we often encounter situations that provoke anger—whether it is injustice, oppression, or wrongdoing. Hanuman's example shows us that anger, when controlled and directed towards a just cause, can be a powerful force for positive change. However, it also reminds us that anger must be tempered with wisdom and self-control. Unchecked anger can lead to destruction and harm, but righteous anger, when guided by a sense of justice and compassion, can help us overcome evil and bring about positive transformation.

Timeliness and Decision Making: The Sanjeevani Mission

One of the most critical moments in the Ramayana is when Lakshmana, Rama's brother, is severely wounded in battle, and the only hope for saving his life is the Sanjeevani herb, which grows on a distant mountain. Hanuman is entrusted with the mission to find and bring back the herb. This task is not just a test of Hanuman's strength and speed, but also of his decision-making abilities.

When Hanuman reaches the mountain where the herb grows, he faces a dilemma. He is unable to identify the Sanjeevani among the many herbs on the mountain. Instead of wasting time trying to figure it out, Hanuman makes a quick decision: he lifts the entire mountain and carries it back to the battlefield. This act not only saves Lakshmana's life but also turns the tide of the war in Rama's favor.

Hanuman's decision to carry the mountain is a brilliant example of quick thinking and decisive action. He understands the urgency of the situation and does not allow himself to be paralyzed by uncertainty. Instead, he takes bold and decisive action, ensuring that the mission is accomplished in time.

This episode offers valuable lessons for all of us, especially in today's fast-paced world where the ability to make quick and effective decisions is often the key to success. Hanuman's example teaches us the importance of decisiveness and the need to take bold action when the situation demands it. It also reminds us that sometimes, the best solution to a problem is not the most obvious or conventional one. By thinking creatively and being willing to take risks, we can find innovative solutions to even the most challenging problems.

Wisdom and Diplomacy: Hanuman's Interaction with Ravana

Throughout the Ramayana, Hanuman displays not only physical strength but also remarkable wisdom and diplomacy. This is particularly evident in his interactions with Ravana and other adversaries. Despite being a fierce warrior, Hanuman understands the value of diplomacy and uses it to great effect in his dealings with Ravana.

When Hanuman is brought before Ravana after being captured, he does not react with anger or violence. Instead, he uses the opportunity to try and reason with Ravana, urging him to return Sita to Rama and avoid the destruction of his kingdom. Hanuman's words are measured and wise, reflecting his deep understanding of human nature and the consequences of Ravana's actions. Even though Ravana ultimately refuses to listen, Hanuman's attempt at diplomacy shows his commitment to peace and his willingness to exhaust all options before resorting to violence.

Hanuman's wisdom is also evident in his ability to assess situations and make strategic decisions. Whether it is deciding how to cross the ocean, how to deal with the demoness Surasa, or how to escape from Ravana's palace, Hanuman consistently demonstrates a keen intellect and a deep understanding of the dynamics at play.

This aspect of Hanuman's character offers important lessons for all of us, particularly in the realm of communication and interpersonal relationships. Hanuman's example teaches us the value of wisdom, diplomacy, and effective communication in resolving conflicts and navigating complex situations. In our own lives, we often encounter challenges that require us to balance strength with wisdom, to assert our position while also seeking to understand and communicate with others. By following Hanuman's example, we can develop the skills needed to navigate these challenges with grace and effectiveness.

Loyalty and Selflessness: The Heart of Hanuman

Perhaps the most defining quality of Hanuman is his unwavering loyalty and selflessness. Throughout the Ramayana, Hanuman consistently puts the needs of others before his own, dedicating himself entirely to the service of Rama. His loyalty is not just a matter of duty; it is a deep, abiding love that drives everything he does.

The ultimate expression of Hanuman's loyalty is the image of Rama that he carries in his heart. According to legend, when someone questioned the depth of Hanuman's devotion, he tore open his chest to reveal the image of Rama and Sita inscribed on his heart. This powerful image symbolizes Hanuman's complete identification with his lord, to the point where his very existence is inseparable from his devotion to Rama.

Hanuman's selflessness is also evident in his actions throughout the Ramayana. Whether it is risking his life to find Sita, lifting the mountain to save Lakshmana, or confronting Ravana in his palace, Hanuman never hesitates to put himself in harm's way for the sake of others. His actions are motivated not by a desire for personal gain or glory, but by a deep sense of duty and love.

This aspect of Hanuman's character offers profound lessons for all of us. In a world where self-interest and individualism often dominate, Hanuman's example reminds us of the importance of loyalty, selflessness, and the power of love. His life teaches us that true greatness lies not in what we achieve for ourselves, but in what we do for others. By following Hanuman's example, we can cultivate a spirit of selflessness and service, leading to deeper, more meaningful relationships and a greater sense of fulfillment in our lives.

Hanuman as a Yogi and Sage

While Hanuman is often celebrated for his physical strength and heroic deeds, he is also revered as a yogi and sage, embodying the highest spiritual ideals of Hinduism. Hanuman's life is a testament to the power of yoga and meditation, and his mastery over his senses and mind is a key aspect of his character.

In Hindu tradition, Hanuman is considered a master of bhakti yoga, the path of devotion, as well as raja yoga, the path of meditation and self-discipline. His unwavering devotion to Rama is the essence of bhakti yoga, where the devotee surrenders completely to the divine, transcending ego and desires. Hanuman's life demonstrates that through devotion and surrender, one can achieve union with the divine and realize the highest spiritual truths.

Hanuman is also depicted as a master of raja yoga, having complete control over his mind and senses. Despite the challenges and temptations he faces, Hanuman remains focused and disciplined, using his inner strength to overcome obstacles and fulfill his mission. His ability to control his anger, fear, and desires reflects his deep spiritual maturity and mastery over the self.

This aspect of Hanuman's character offers valuable lessons for those on the spiritual path. In our own lives, we often struggle with the challenges of controlling our minds and emotions, and finding balance and peace in a chaotic world. Hanuman's example teaches us the importance of spiritual discipline, meditation, and devotion in achieving inner peace and self-mastery. By following Hanuman's example, we can develop the spiritual strength and wisdom needed to navigate life's challenges and achieve a deeper connection with the divine.

The Relevance of Hanuman in the Modern World

Hanuman's life and teachings are not just relevant to ancient times; they offer timeless wisdom that is highly applicable in the modern world. In today's fast-paced, competitive, and often stressful environment, the qualities that Hanuman embodies—devotion, strength, humility, wisdom, and selflessness—are more important than ever.

In the workplace, Hanuman's example of loyalty, dedication, and teamwork can inspire us to be better employees and leaders, fostering a spirit of cooperation and mutual support. In our personal lives, his qualities of devotion, humility, and selflessness can help us build stronger, more meaningful relationships with our families, friends, and communities.

Hanuman's ability to overcome obstacles and face challenges with courage and determination is particularly relevant in today's world, where many of us face significant challenges in our careers, relationships, and personal lives. By drawing inspiration from Hanuman's life, we can find the strength and resilience needed to overcome these challenges and achieve our goals.

Moreover, Hanuman's example of balance—between strength and humility, action and wisdom, self-discipline and devotion—offers a valuable model for achieving balance in our own lives. In a world that often pulls us in multiple directions, Hanuman's life teaches us the importance of staying grounded, focused, and true to our principles, while also remaining open to growth and change.

Conclusion

In conclusion, Lord Hanuman is much more than a mythological figure; he is a symbol of the highest human and spiritual ideals. His life and teachings offer profound lessons that are relevant to every aspect of our lives, from our personal and professional relationships to our spiritual growth and development. By studying and emulating Hanuman's qualities, we can cultivate the strength, wisdom, and devotion needed to navigate life's challenges and fulfill our highest potential.

Hanuman's story is a testament to the power of devotion, the strength of humility, the wisdom of self-control, and the importance of selfless service. His life teaches us that true greatness lies not in our achievements, but in our ability to serve others, to overcome challenges with courage and determination, and to remain true to our principles and values. In a world that often values power, wealth, and status, Hanuman's example reminds us of the deeper, more enduring values that lead to true fulfillment and happiness.

As we continue to face the challenges and opportunities of the modern world, Hanuman's life and teachings will continue to serve as a source of inspiration and guidance, helping us to navigate the complexities of life with strength, wisdom, and grace.

CHAPTER II

The Birth and Early Life of Hanuman

Origins of Devotion: The Miraculous Birth and Formative Years of the Mighty Vanara

The story of Lord Hanuman begins with a confluence of divine forces and cosmic events that set the stage for his birth, which is not just a birth of a being, but of a legend that would stand as an eternal symbol of strength, devotion, and unwavering faith. To understand Hanuman's significance and his later exploits, it is crucial to delve deeply into the circumstances surrounding his birth and the early years of his life. These formative years laid the foundation for the qualities that would define him throughout the epic of the Ramayana and beyond.

The Divine Conception

Hanuman's birth is a narrative interwoven with divinity, reflecting the profound interconnection between the gods, the cosmos, and the earthly realm. His mother, Anjana, was not an ordinary being; she was a celestial nymph, known as an apsara, who was cursed to live on earth as a vanara, a being that is part monkey and part human. This curse, however, was not a random act of fate. It was part of a grander cosmic design, orchestrated by the gods to prepare for the arrival of a being who would play a pivotal role in the battle between good and evil.

Anjana's transformation from a heavenly apsara to a mortal vanara is itself a story steeped in symbolism. The apsaras, who were known for their beauty, grace, and ability to enchant, represented the ethereal and transient aspects of existence. Their lives in the heavens were marked by joy and pleasure, unburdened by the trials and tribulations of the earthly realm. Anjana's fall from this heavenly state to the earth as a vanara reflects a descent from the divine to the mortal, from the ethereal to the material. However, this descent was not a punishment but a necessary step in the fulfillment of a divine mission.

The curse that transformed Anjana into a vanara was also her path to redemption. As a vanara, she married Kesari, a powerful and righteous leader of the vanara community. Kesari was known for his strength, valor, and unwavering commitment to dharma, the moral law that governs the universe. The union of Anjana and Kesari symbolized the coming together of divine beauty and earthly strength, a union that would give birth to Hanuman, a being who embodied both these qualities in their highest form.

The most critical element in Hanuman's conception, however, was the involvement of Vayu, the god of wind. Vayu, who is also referred to as the breath of life, is one of the most powerful and omnipresent deities in Hindu mythology. His presence signifies the life force that animates all living beings, the invisible power that moves through the universe, connecting all things. According to the legend, Anjana was deep in meditation, performing penance to be freed from her curse and to regain her heavenly form. Pleased with her devotion, the god Vayu, acting on the will of Lord Shiva, blessed her with a son who would possess extraordinary powers.

It is said that while Anjana was praying, she received the divine blessing from Vayu, who infused her with his essence. This act of divine intervention led to the birth of Hanuman, who inherited the qualities of his celestial parents. From Anjana, Hanuman received grace, beauty, and the ability to enchant others. From Kesari, he inherited strength, valor, and a deep sense of duty. And from Vayu, Hanuman inherited the ability to move swiftly, the power to transcend physical limitations, and an indomitable spirit.

This confluence of divine elements in Hanuman's birth is not just a fascinating story but also a symbolic representation of the forces that shape our lives. Hanuman's birth teaches us that we are all the product of multiple influences—divine, natural, and human.

Just as Hanuman inherited different qualities from his parents, we too inherit various traits, abilities, and tendencies from the different forces in our lives. The story of Hanuman's birth reminds us of the potential within each of us to harness these influences and rise to our highest potential.

Hanuman's Childhood: A Mischievous Divine Child

Hanuman's early life is filled with tales of his boundless energy, curiosity, and mischievous nature, traits that are typical of a young child but are magnified in Hanuman due to his divine heritage. His childhood was marked by his constant exploration of the world around him, driven by an insatiable curiosity and an innate sense of wonder. However, unlike ordinary children, Hanuman's explorations often led to extraordinary events, reflecting his divine nature.

One of the most famous episodes from Hanuman's childhood is the story of his attempt to eat the sun. This tale is not just a charming anecdote but is rich with symbolic meaning. According to the legend, one day, the young Hanuman saw the sun rising in the sky and, mistaking it for a ripe fruit, leaped into the sky to catch it. The sight of a tiny monkey leaping towards the sun is both humorous and awe-inspiring, illustrating Hanuman's fearless nature and his tendency to see the world through the lens of his boundless curiosity.

As Hanuman soared towards the sun, the gods in the heavens were thrown into a state of alarm. The sun, after all, was not just a celestial body but a vital force in the universe, and Hanuman's attempt to swallow it could have catastrophic consequences. Indra, the king of the gods, tried to stop Hanuman by striking him with his thunderbolt, the Vajra. The impact of the Vajra struck Hanuman on the jaw, causing him to fall back to earth. This event led to his name, "Hanuman," which is derived from the Sanskrit words "hanu," meaning jaw, and "man," meaning disfigured or injured.

The story of Hanuman's attempt to eat the sun is symbolic on multiple levels. The sun represents the ultimate source of energy and life in the universe, and Hanuman's attempt to grasp it reflects the human desire to reach for the highest, to attain the unattainable. His fall back to earth, caused by Indra's Vajra, symbolizes the limitations that are inherent in the human condition—the obstacles and challenges that prevent us from reaching our goals. However, Hanuman's story also carries a message of resilience and the potential for growth. Despite being struck down, Hanuman did not lose his spirit or his divine nature. Instead, the incident became a part of his journey, teaching him the importance of humility and self-restraint.

This episode also highlights the relationship between Hanuman and the gods, particularly Vayu, his divine father. When Vayu saw his son injured and unconscious after being struck by Indra's thunderbolt, he was filled with anger and sorrow. In his grief, Vayu withdrew his presence from the world, causing all living beings to suffocate and the winds to cease. The gods, realizing the gravity of the situation, rushed to appease Vayu and to revive Hanuman. They blessed Hanuman with numerous boons, each conferring upon him extraordinary powers. Brahma, the creator, granted Hanuman immunity from all weapons; Indra blessed him with a life free from the fear of death; and Surya, the sun god, bestowed upon him wisdom and knowledge.

These blessings not only restored Hanuman but also elevated him to a status that was far beyond that of any ordinary being. The gods recognized in Hanuman a potential that would play a crucial role in the cosmic balance, and they equipped him with the tools necessary to fulfill his destiny. The incident also deepened the bond between Hanuman and his divine father, Vayu, highlighting the theme of divine intervention and protection that would recur throughout Hanuman's life.

Hanuman's Education: Learning from the Sun God

Another significant chapter in Hanuman's early life is his education under Surya, the sun god. After the incident with the sun, Surya became not just a benefactor to Hanuman but also his teacher. This relationship is unique and profound, as it symbolizes the transmission of divine knowledge and wisdom to a being who would later become an embodiment of both physical strength and intellectual prowess.

According to the legends, Hanuman, eager to learn and grow, approached Surya and requested him to be his teacher. Surya, who was constantly moving across the sky, initially hesitated, explaining that his duties required him to be in perpetual motion and that he would not have the time to teach Hanuman. However, Hanuman, undeterred by this challenge, offered to follow Surya throughout the day, absorbing his teachings as they traveled across the heavens.

This episode highlights Hanuman's determination and his thirst for knowledge. His willingness to follow Surya and learn while in motion reflects his adaptability and his ability to overcome obstacles through sheer will and persistence. It also symbolizes the idea that true knowledge requires effort, dedication, and the willingness to go beyond conventional boundaries.

Under Surya's tutelage, Hanuman learned the Vedas, the ancient scriptures that contain the wisdom of the universe. He also mastered various arts and sciences, becoming proficient in grammar, logic, and the esoteric knowledge of the cosmos. Surya, impressed by Hanuman's dedication and intellectual brilliance, offered him a boon. However, Hanuman, in his characteristic humility, refused any material reward. Instead, he asked Surya to accept his service as payment for the knowledge he had received.

This act of humility and selflessness is a defining moment in Hanuman's life. It shows that for Hanuman, the pursuit of knowledge was not motivated by a desire for power or recognition but by a genuine desire to grow and serve. His refusal to accept a boon from Surya also reflects his deep understanding of dharma, the moral law that governs the universe. Hanuman recognized that true knowledge is its own reward and that the highest form of service is the selfless dedication to one's duties and responsibilities.

The relationship between Hanuman and Surya is also symbolic of the transmission of divine knowledge from the source of light and life to a being destined to illuminate the world with his wisdom and strength. Surya, the sun god, represents the ultimate source of enlightenment, and Hanuman, as his student, becomes a vessel for this divine light. This relationship underscores the importance of seeking out and respecting sources of wisdom and knowledge in our own lives. It reminds us that true learning is a lifelong journey that requires humility, dedication, and a willingness to serve.

The Curse and the Boon: Hanuman's Forgetfulness

Despite the divine powers and knowledge that Hanuman acquired in his early years, his journey was not without its trials. One of the most significant events in his early life was the curse of forgetfulness that was placed upon him by the sages he inadvertently disturbed with his playful antics.

As a child, Hanuman's boundless energy and mischievous nature often led him to cause disruptions. His pranks, though innocent, were powerful due to his divine strength and abilities. One such incident involved Hanuman playfully interfering with the meditations of a group of rishis (sages). Frustrated by his constant interruptions, the sages decided to curb Hanuman's powers by placing a curse on him. They decreed that Hanuman would forget his own strength and abilities until someone reminded him of them in the context of a great mission.

This curse, while seemingly punitive, was actually a blessing in disguise. By making Hanuman forget his powers, the sages ensured that he would not misuse them in his childhood or out of sheer mischief. Instead, Hanuman's powers would be preserved and would emerge only when they were truly needed—in the service of Lord Rama and in the battle against evil.

The curse of forgetfulness also serves as a profound metaphor for the human condition. Just as Hanuman forgets his own divine nature, we too often forget our own potential and the divine spark within us. We go through life unaware of the immense power and wisdom that lie dormant within us, waiting to be awakened. Hanuman's story reminds us that our true potential may be hidden, but it is never lost. It can be reawakened at the right moment, through the right circumstances and with the right guidance.

This aspect of Hanuman's life also introduces the theme of destiny and divine timing. Hanuman's powers were destined to manifest at a crucial moment in the Ramayana, and the curse ensured that they would remain latent until that moment arrived. This teaches us that everything in life happens according to a divine plan, and sometimes what seems like a setback or limitation is actually part of a larger design.

The Transition to Adulthood: Hanuman's Role Among the Vanaras

As Hanuman grew from a mischievous child into a young adult, his role within the vanara community also evolved. The vanaras, a race of beings with both human and monkey-like characteristics, were known for their strength, agility, and loyalty. They lived in the forests and mountains of Kishkindha, a kingdom ruled by the vanara king Sugriva. The vanaras played a significant role in the Ramayana, and Hanuman, with his unique abilities and divine heritage, became one of their most important leaders.

Hanuman's transition into adulthood was marked by a growing awareness of his responsibilities and his role within the larger cosmic order. Unlike his early years, where his actions were driven by curiosity and playfulness, Hanuman as a young adult began to embody the qualities of a leader and a warrior. His loyalty to Sugriva, the exiled vanara king, and his role in the conflict between Sugriva and his brother Vali, marked the beginning of Hanuman's emergence as a key figure in the unfolding epic.

The conflict between Sugriva and Vali is one of the most significant episodes in the Ramayana and serves as a backdrop for Hanuman's early adulthood. Vali, the elder brother of Sugriva, had unjustly seized the throne of Kishkindha and exiled Sugriva. Despite being stronger than his brother, Vali was also arrogant and ruthless, qualities that eventually led to his downfall. Sugriva, on the other hand, was righteous but lacked the power to challenge Vali. It was in this context that Hanuman's loyalty and strategic acumen came to the fore.

Hanuman, recognizing the injustice done to Sugriva, became his loyal supporter and advisor. He played a crucial role in forging the alliance between Sugriva and Lord Rama, an alliance that would eventually lead to the defeat of Vali and the restoration of Sugriva to the throne. Hanuman's role in this conflict highlights his qualities of loyalty, wisdom, and strategic thinking. He was not just a warrior, but a statesman and a diplomat, capable of navigating the complex dynamics of power and politics.

The episode of Vali and Sugriva also serves as a reminder of the importance of dharma, or righteousness, in leadership. Vali, despite his strength, fell because he strayed from the path of dharma, while Sugriva, with the support of Hanuman and Rama, was restored to his rightful place because he represented righteousness. Hanuman's involvement in this conflict underscores his deep commitment to dharma and his willingness to stand by those who are just and righteous, even in the face of great danger.

Hanuman and the Search for Sita

One of the most important and defining moments in Hanuman's early adulthood is his role in the search for Sita, Lord Rama's wife, who was abducted by the demon king Ravana. This mission not only tested Hanuman's strength and abilities but also marked the beginning of his deep and unwavering devotion to Rama.

The search for Sita was a monumental task, fraught with dangers and uncertainties. Ravana, the king of Lanka, had taken Sita to his island fortress, which was surrounded by vast oceans and guarded by powerful demons. The task of finding Sita required a combination of physical strength, intelligence, and divine intervention. It was in this context that Hanuman's true potential began to manifest.

Hanuman's role in the search for Sita is perhaps one of the most celebrated episodes in the Ramayana. His journey across the ocean to Lanka, his encounters with various obstacles and challenges, and his eventual discovery of Sita in Ravana's palace, all demonstrate the qualities that make Hanuman a revered figure in Hindu mythology.

The journey to Lanka was not just a physical journey but also a spiritual one. Hanuman, who had been cursed with forgetfulness, was reminded of his true nature and powers by Jambavan, the wise elder of the vanaras. This moment of awakening is crucial, as it marks the point where Hanuman fully realizes his potential and steps into his role as a divine hero. His leap across the ocean, often depicted as one of the most iconic images in Hindu art and literature, symbolizes the overcoming of obstacles through faith, courage, and determination.

During his journey, Hanuman encountered several challenges, each representing different aspects of human experience. The encounter with the demoness Surasa, who tried to devour him, symbolizes the struggle against fear and ignorance. Hanuman's ability to outwit Surasa by shrinking his size and entering her mouth, only to emerge unscathed, represents the triumph of wisdom and intelligence over brute force and fear.

The encounter with Simhika, a demoness who tried to capture Hanuman by grabbing his shadow, symbolizes the struggle against the forces of illusion and attachment. Hanuman's ability to defeat Simhika by recognizing her true nature and striking her down represents the importance of discernment and clarity in overcoming obstacles.

Finally, Hanuman's arrival in Lanka and his search for Sita within the city's fortifications symbolize the search for truth and the ultimate goal of the spiritual journey. Hanuman's discovery of Sita, imprisoned and sorrowful in Ravana's Garden, is a moment of deep emotional and spiritual significance. It is here that Hanuman's role as a messenger and servant of Rama is fully realized. His compassion for Sita, his willingness to offer her comfort and hope, and his commitment to ensuring her safety, all reflect the qualities of devotion, empathy, and service that define Hanuman's character.

The search for Sita also highlights Hanuman's role as a bridge between the human and divine realms. His ability to traverse the physical and spiritual worlds, to communicate with beings of both realms, and to act as a mediator between Rama and Sita, underscores his unique position in the Ramayana. Hanuman is not just a warrior or a devotee; he is a link between the earthly and the divine, a being who embodies the highest ideals of both.

Conclusion

The birth and early life of Hanuman are more than just the origin story of a mythological hero. They are a profound exploration of the forces that shape us, the challenges that define us, and the potential that lies within us. Hanuman's journey from a mischievous child to a divine hero is a story of growth, learning, and the awakening of inner strength.

Hanuman's early life teaches us about the importance of humility, devotion, and the pursuit of knowledge. It reminds us that our true potential may be hidden, but it is always present, waiting to be awakened. Hanuman's story also highlights the importance of dharma, the moral law that guides our actions, and the role of divine intervention in our lives.

As we explore the later chapters of Hanuman's life, we will see how these early experiences shaped him into the legendary figure he became—an embodiment of strength, wisdom, and devotion, whose story continues to inspire millions of people around the world.

CHAPTER III

Hanuman's Devotion to Lord Rama

The Embodiment of Bhakti: Unwavering Loyalty and Love for His Divine Master

Hanuman's devotion to Lord Rama stands as one of the most exemplary tales of unwavering loyalty, selfless service, and pure love in the entire expanse of Hindu mythology. This devotion is not merely the affection of a disciple towards his teacher, or a follower towards a leader; it is a profound, soul-deep bond that transcends the ordinary relationships of the world. Hanuman's entire being—his thoughts, actions, and existence—is centered around Rama, making his devotion a spiritual force that has inspired countless generations.

To understand Hanuman's devotion, it is essential to explore the depths of his character, the circumstances that led to his first encounter with Rama, and the significant events that solidified his role as Rama's most ardent devotee. This chapter delves into the various facets of Hanuman's devotion, his interactions with Rama, and the lessons they impart to us about faith, loyalty, and the path of bhakti (devotion).

The First Meeting: A Cosmic Union

The first meeting between Hanuman and Lord Rama is a pivotal moment in the Ramayana and serves as the foundation of their relationship. This meeting, however, was not a mere coincidence; it was the fulfillment of a cosmic plan, orchestrated by the divine forces to bring together two beings whose destinies were intertwined.

According to the Ramayana, after Sita was abducted by Ravana, Rama and his brother Lakshmana began their search for her. Their journey led them to the region of Kishkindha, where they encountered the exiled vanara king, Sugriva. It was during this time that Hanuman, a loyal minister and confidant of Sugriva, first came into contact with Rama.

The encounter between Hanuman and Rama is rich with symbolism. Disguised as a simple ascetic, Hanuman approached Rama and Lakshmana with humility and reverence, not yet fully aware of their divine nature. However, the moment Hanuman laid eyes on Rama, something profound stirred within him. His soul recognized the divinity of Rama, even before his mind could fully comprehend it. This recognition was not based on physical appearance or external signs but on a deep, intuitive understanding of Rama's true nature.

Hanuman's first words to Rama were a blend of courtesy and wisdom, reflecting his deep understanding and his role as an emissary of Sugriva. He introduced himself as Sugriva's servant and offered his assistance to Rama, demonstrating his readiness to serve without hesitation. Rama, in turn, was struck by Hanuman's intelligence, eloquence, and humility. The bond that formed between them in this first meeting was immediate and unbreakable, setting the stage for the many adventures that would follow.

This initial encounter between Hanuman and Rama highlights the concept of divine recognition, where the soul instinctively recognizes and is drawn to the divine presence. Hanuman's instant devotion to Rama is symbolic of the innate spiritual longing within every being—the yearning to connect with the divine, which, once awakened, becomes the driving force behind all actions.

The Unwavering Loyalty: Hanuman's Role in the Ramayana

Hanuman's role in the Ramayana is not just that of a devotee but of a protector, messenger, and warrior. His devotion to Rama is expressed through his actions, each of which is marked by a deep sense of loyalty and dedication. Unlike other characters in the Ramayana who might be driven by personal motives or external rewards, Hanuman's actions are purely driven by his desire to serve Rama and fulfill his divine mission.

One of the most significant demonstrations of Hanuman's loyalty is his journey to Lanka in search of Sita. After forging an alliance between Rama and Sugriva, it was decided that the vanaras would search for Sita, who had been taken by Ravana to his fortress in Lanka. This mission was fraught with challenges and dangers, but Hanuman took it upon himself to find Sita, driven by his unwavering devotion to Rama.

Hanuman's leap across the ocean to reach Lanka is one of the most iconic episodes in the Ramayana. The ocean, a vast and seemingly insurmountable obstacle, symbolizes the challenges and difficulties that one must overcome in the path of devotion. Hanuman, by invoking Rama's name and relying on his faith, was able to accomplish what seemed impossible. His leap across the ocean is a metaphor for the power of devotion to transcend limitations and overcome even the greatest obstacles.

Upon reaching Lanka, Hanuman faced numerous challenges, including the fierce guardians and the formidable defenses of Ravana's palace. However, driven by his devotion to Rama and his determination to find Sita, Hanuman navigated these obstacles with intelligence, courage, and a deep sense of purpose. His encounter with Sita in the Ashoka grove, where she was held captive, is a moment of profound emotional and spiritual significance.

When Hanuman finally found Sita, he approached her with the utmost respect and humility. He identified himself as Rama's messenger and offered her the reassurance of Rama's love and commitment to rescuing her. This moment is deeply symbolic, as Hanuman acts as the bridge between the despairing Sita and the hopeful Rama. His role as a messenger is not just a physical task but a spiritual mission, as he brings the light of hope and the promise of deliverance to Sita, who had been languishing in captivity.

The episode of Hanuman's encounter with Sita also highlights his wisdom and understanding of the human condition. He recognized Sita's deep sorrow and her unwavering faith in Rama, and he responded with compassion and empathy. By offering her Rama's ring as a token of his love, Hanuman not only reassured Sita but also solidified his role as the link between the divine and the mortal. This act of service, driven by devotion, is a testament to the power of selfless love and the importance of faith in overcoming adversity.

Hanuman's return from Lanka, carrying Sita's message for Rama, further underscores his role as a devoted servant. Despite the dangers he faced, including his capture and the destruction of part of Lanka, Hanuman's only concern was to fulfill his mission and bring back news of Sita to Rama. His actions throughout this journey are marked by a single-minded focus on Rama's well-being, demonstrating the depth of his loyalty and his commitment to Rama's cause.

Hanuman's Devotion and the War in Lanka

The war in Lanka is the climax of the Ramayana and a period where Hanuman's devotion to Rama is most evident. As the battle between Rama's forces and Ravana's army unfolded, Hanuman emerged not just as a warrior but as a symbol of divine strength and devotion. His actions during the war, particularly his unwavering support for Rama and his role in key events, highlight the transformative power of bhakti.

One of the most famous episodes during the war is Hanuman's journey to the Himalayas to retrieve the Sanjeevani herb. This event is a powerful testament to Hanuman's devotion and his role as a savior. During the battle, Lakshmana was struck by a powerful arrow from Ravana's son, Indrajit, and fell unconscious. Rama, stricken with grief, was told that Lakshmana could only be saved by the Sanjeevani herb, found in the Dronagiri mountain in the Himalayas. Hanuman was tasked with retrieving this life-saving herb.

The journey to the Himalayas was not just a test of Hanuman's strength but of his devotion and determination. He faced numerous challenges along the way, including the difficulty of finding the exact herb among the myriad plants on the mountain. However, Hanuman's devotion to Rama and his love for Lakshmana drove him to overcome these challenges. In his desperation to save Lakshmana, Hanuman lifted the entire mountain and carried it back to the battlefield, ensuring that the herb could be found and administered in time.

This episode is symbolic of the lengths to which true devotion will go to serve the divine. Hanuman's act of carrying the mountain is not just a demonstration of physical strength but of the power of love and devotion to move mountains—literally and figuratively. It highlights the idea that when one is driven by pure devotion, no obstacle is too great, and no task is impossible.

Throughout the war, Hanuman's actions were consistently driven by his desire to support Rama and ensure the victory of dharma (righteousness) over adharma (unrighteousness). Whether it was by leading the vanara army, engaging in combat with formidable foes, or providing crucial support in moments of crisis, Hanuman's every action was motivated by his devotion to Rama. His presence on the battlefield was not just that of a warrior but of a protector and guardian of Rama and his mission.

The Pinnacle of Devotion: Hanuman's Service to Rama

Beyond the battlefield, Hanuman's devotion to Rama manifested in countless acts of service, both great and small. Unlike other devotees who might seek recognition or rewards for their service, Hanuman's devotion was marked by complete selflessness. His only desire was to serve Rama, and his greatest joy came from fulfilling Rama's wishes.

One of the most touching aspects of Hanuman's devotion is his humility. Despite his extraordinary powers and the pivotal role he played in the Ramayana, Hanuman never sought glory or recognition for himself. He always considered himself a servant of Rama, and his actions were driven by the desire to please his lord rather than to achieve personal greatness. This humility is exemplified in his interactions with Rama, where he consistently placed Rama's happiness and well-being above his own.

After the war in Lanka and the defeat of Ravana, Hanuman continued to serve Rama with the same devotion. When Rama, Sita, and Lakshmana returned to Ayodhya and were crowned, Hanuman remained by their side, ever ready to serve. His devotion was not limited to the extraordinary feats he performed during the war but extended to the simple, everyday acts of service that defined his relationship with Rama.

Hanuman's devotion also extended to Sita, whom he revered as the divine consort of Rama. His respect for Sita is evident in his actions, particularly during the events following the war. When Rama doubted Sita's purity after her captivity in Lanka, it was Hanuman who stood by her and supported her during this difficult time. His respect for Sita was rooted in his understanding of her divine nature and his unwavering belief in her righteousness.

One of the most profound moments that illustrate Hanuman's devotion is the scene where Rama tests Hanuman's loyalty by offering him a reward. After the successful completion of the mission to rescue Sita and defeat Ravana, Rama offered Hanuman a boon, asking him to name any reward he desired. Hanuman, however, did not ask for wealth, power, or even liberation (moksha). Instead, he asked only for the blessing that he could continue to serve Rama in all his lifetimes. This selfless request encapsulates the essence of Hanuman's devotion—a love that seeks nothing in return, except the opportunity to continue serving the beloved.

Hanuman's request to remain forever in the service of Rama is a powerful expression of the concept of eternal devotion. It reflects the idea that true devotion transcends the limitations of time and space, continuing even beyond death and rebirth. Hanuman's desire to remain by Rama's side, in whatever form or capacity, is a testament to the depth of his love and the purity of his devotion.

Hanuman as the Ideal Devotee: Lessons from His Bhakti

Hanuman's devotion to Rama is not just a story from ancient mythology but a timeless example of the ideal devotee. His life and actions provide valuable lessons on the nature of devotion, the importance of selfless service, and the transformative power of love.

One of the key lessons from Hanuman's devotion is the idea of **selfless service**. Hanuman's every action was motivated by his desire to serve Rama, without any expectation of reward or recognition. This selflessness is a hallmark of true devotion, where the devotee's focus is entirely on the beloved, and personal desires and ego are set aside. Hanuman's example teaches us that true happiness and fulfillment come not from seeking personal gains but from serving others and fulfilling our higher purpose.

Another important lesson from Hanuman's devotion is the power of **faith**. Hanuman's faith in Rama was unshakeable, even in the face of the most daunting challenges. This faith gave him the strength to overcome obstacles, perform miraculous feats, and remain steadfast in his service to Rama. Hanuman's story reminds us that faith is a powerful force that can help us navigate the difficulties of life and stay true to our path.

Humility is another virtue that shines through in Hanuman's devotion. Despite his extraordinary powers and accomplishments, Hanuman never saw himself as superior to others. He always considered himself a humble servant of Rama, and his actions were driven by a deep sense of humility. This humility is a reminder that true greatness lies not in seeking praise or recognition but in serving others with a pure heart.

Hanuman's devotion also illustrates the importance of **loyalty** and **dedication**. Once Hanuman recognized Rama as his lord, he remained unwaveringly loyal to him, even in the face of danger and adversity. This loyalty was not just a matter of duty but a reflection of Hanuman's deep love and commitment to Rama. Hanuman's example teaches us the value of staying true to our commitments and being loyal to the people and principles we hold dear.

Finally, Hanuman's devotion highlights the concept of **eternal love**. His love for Rama was not limited by time or circumstances; it was an eternal bond that transcended all boundaries. Hanuman's desire to remain in Rama's service for all eternity reflects the idea that true love is everlasting and that the bond between the devotee and the divine is unbreakable.

Conclusion: The Enduring Legacy of Hanuman's Devotion

Hanuman's devotion to Lord Rama is a story of unparalleled love, loyalty, and selfless service. It is a story that has been passed down through the ages, inspiring countless devotees and serving as a model of ideal devotion. Hanuman's life and actions demonstrate that true devotion is not about rituals or external displays of faith but about a deep, inner connection with the divine.

The legacy of Hanuman's devotion continues to resonate with people of all backgrounds, offering a powerful example of how love and service can transcend the limitations of the human condition. Hanuman's story reminds us that the path of devotion is not just about worship but about living a life of selflessness, humility, and unwavering faith.

In the end, Hanuman's devotion to Rama is a testament to the transformative power of love—a love that is pure, unconditional, and eternal. It is a love that inspires us to look beyond our own desires and to dedicate ourselves to a higher purpose. Through his devotion, Hanuman became more than just a servant of Rama; he became a symbol of divine love, a beacon of faith, and an embodiment of the highest ideals of devotion.

As we reflect on Hanuman's devotion, we are reminded that the path of bhakti is open to all, regardless of who we are or where we come from. Hanuman's story invites us to cultivate the same qualities of love, faith, and service in our own lives, and to strive towards a deeper connection with the divine. In doing so, we can find the strength to overcome our own challenges, the wisdom to navigate the complexities of life, and the peace that comes from living in harmony with our higher purpose.

CHAPTER IV

The Power of Humility and Strength

Lessons in Balance: How True Power Resides in the Humble and the Compassionate

The narrative of Hanuman in the Ramayana is a profound exploration of the dual forces of humility and strength, which, when combined, form a compelling model for leadership, service, and spiritual growth. Hanuman is an embodiment of physical power and intellectual prowess, yet his greatest strength lies in his humility—a virtue that defines his character and amplifies his other abilities. This chapter delves into the deep interplay between humility and strength in Hanuman's life, examining how these qualities complement each other, how they manifest in his actions, and what they teach us about the true nature of power.

Understanding Humility: The Foundation of Hanuman's Character

Humility, in the context of Hanuman, is not merely the absence of pride; it is an active, dynamic quality that governs his thoughts, actions, and relationships. It is the recognition of one's abilities and strengths, coupled with the awareness that these gifts are not for self-aggrandizement but for the service of others and the divine will. Hanuman's humility is deeply rooted in his spiritual understanding and his unwavering devotion to Lord Rama.

From the very beginning, Hanuman's humility is evident in his interactions with others. Despite being born with incredible powers, Hanuman does not flaunt his abilities or seek to dominate others. He approaches every situation with a sense of reverence and a desire to serve. This humility is not a sign of weakness but a conscious choice to place the needs of others above his own, and to use his strength in the service of a higher purpose.

Hanuman's humility is also reflected in his self-perception. He does not see himself as a great hero or a divine being, but as a humble servant of Rama. This self-concept is central to his identity and drives all his actions. Even after performing extraordinary feats, Hanuman remains grounded, attributing his successes to Rama's grace rather than his own abilities. This humility, combined with his unwavering faith, is what makes Hanuman such a powerful and inspiring figure.

A key aspect of Hanuman's humility is his lack of ego. Unlike many other characters in the Ramayana who are driven by pride, ambition, or a desire for recognition, Hanuman's actions are free from any sense of self-importance. He does not seek glory or rewards for his deeds; his only concern is to fulfill his duty and serve Rama. This absence of ego allows Hanuman to act with clarity and purpose, unclouded by personal desires or attachments.

In the episode where Hanuman leaps across the ocean to reach Lanka, his humility is particularly striking. Despite the enormity of the task and the magnitude of his accomplishment, Hanuman does not boast or take pride in his achievement. Instead, he offers his success as a humble offering to Rama, acknowledging that it is Rama's power and blessings that enabled him to complete the mission. This humility is what makes Hanuman's strength so potent—he uses it not for self-glorification but for the greater good.

Hanuman's humility is further exemplified in his interactions with Sita in Lanka. When he finally locates Sita in the Ashoka grove, Hanuman approaches her with deep respect and reverence. Despite his eagerness to reassure her and deliver Rama's message, Hanuman does not rush or impose himself upon her. He patiently waits for the right moment to reveal himself, understanding the delicate nature of the situation and Sita's emotional state. This sensitivity and respect for others' feelings are hallmarks of true humility.

Even in his later years, when Hanuman becomes a revered figure and a symbol of devotion, he never loses his humility. He continues to see himself as a servant of Rama, dedicated to fulfilling his lord's will. This enduring humility is what makes Hanuman's character so timeless and relatable. It is a reminder that true greatness lies not in one's achievements or power, but in the ability to remain humble and selfless in the face of success.

Strength as a Divine Gift: Hanuman's Power and Its Purpose

Hanuman's physical and intellectual strength is legendary. From his childhood, where he playfully soared through the skies and attempted to swallow the sun, to his heroic feats in the Ramayana, Hanuman's strength is a central theme of his character. However, Hanuman's strength is not merely a physical attribute; it is deeply intertwined with his spiritual understanding and his role as a divine instrument.

Hanuman's strength is depicted as limitless and boundless, capable of overcoming any obstacle or enemy. This strength is not just a result of his divine parentage, but also of his unwavering devotion to Rama. In many instances, Hanuman's strength is portrayed as a direct manifestation of Rama's power. It is his faith in Rama that enables Hanuman to perform extraordinary feats, such as lifting mountains, leaping across oceans, and defeating powerful demons.

One of the most significant aspects of Hanuman's strength is that it is always used for a higher purpose. Unlike many mythological figures whose strength leads to arrogance or tyranny, Hanuman's power is tempered by his humility and his commitment to dharma (righteousness). He uses his strength not for personal gain, but to protect the weak, serve the divine will, and uphold justice. This selfless use of power is what sets Hanuman apart from other heroes and makes his strength truly admirable.

Hanuman's strength is also closely linked to his spiritual discipline and his mastery over his senses. Unlike many other characters in the Ramayana who are driven by their desires or emotions, Hanuman is able to control his impulses and channel his energy towards his goals. This self-mastery is a key aspect of his strength, as it allows him to remain focused and undistracted, even in the most challenging situations. Hanuman's strength is thus not just physical, but also mental and spiritual, rooted in his inner discipline and his alignment with the divine will.

The episode of Hanuman carrying the Sanjeevani mountain is a powerful illustration of his strength and its divine purpose. When Lakshmana is struck down by Indrajit, Hanuman is tasked with finding the Sanjeevani herb to revive him. Despite the daunting nature of the task, Hanuman remains undeterred, driven by his love for Rama and his desire to save Lakshmana. His strength enables him to lift the entire mountain and carry it back to the battlefield, a feat that would be impossible for anyone else. This episode is a testament to the power of strength when it is guided by love and devotion.

Hanuman's strength is also evident in his combat abilities. During the war in Lanka, Hanuman single-handedly defeats numerous demons and plays a crucial role in the victory of Rama's forces. His strength is portrayed as both formidable and unstoppable, capable of turning the tide of battle. However, even in the heat of battle, Hanuman's strength is never used recklessly or without purpose. He fights with a sense of duty and righteousness, using his power to protect the innocent and punish the wicked.

Another important aspect of Hanuman's strength is its connection to his knowledge and wisdom. Hanuman is not just a warrior, but also a scholar and a wise counselor. His knowledge of the Vedas, his understanding of dharma, and his strategic acumen are all integral to his strength. This combination of physical power and intellectual prowess makes Hanuman a truly formidable figure. His strength is not just about brute force, but also about the ability to think, plan, and act in accordance with the divine will.

Hanuman's strength is also symbolic of the power of devotion. His feats are not just demonstrations of physical might, but expressions of his deep love for Rama. It is his devotion that gives Hanuman the strength to overcome any obstacle and achieve the impossible. This idea of strength as a manifestation of devotion is a central theme in Hanuman's story and one of the reasons why he is revered as the epitome of bhakti.

The Interplay of Humility and Strength: Hanuman's Unique Power

The most remarkable aspect of Hanuman's character is the seamless integration of humility and strength. In Hanuman, these two qualities are not in conflict but work together to create a powerful and balanced personality. His humility does not diminish his strength; rather, it enhances it by ensuring that his power is used wisely and selflessly. Similarly, his strength does not lead to arrogance; instead, it is tempered by his humility, which keeps his ego in check and his actions aligned with the divine will.

This interplay of humility and strength is evident in many aspects of Hanuman's life. For example, in his interactions with Rama, Hanuman always approaches with deep respect and reverence, despite his immense power. He never assumes an air of superiority or tries to impose his will on Rama. Instead, he remains humble, recognizing that his strength is a gift from the divine and that his role is to serve, not to dominate. This humility allows Hanuman to be a true instrument of Rama's will, using his strength to fulfill the divine mission.

Similarly, in his dealings with other characters in the Ramayana, Hanuman's humility is always present, even in situations where his strength gives him a clear advantage. For example, when he meets Ravana, Hanuman does not boast or threaten, despite knowing that he has the power to defeat him. Instead, he approaches Ravana with a sense of purpose and righteousness, using his strength to convey the message of dharma rather than to assert his own superiority.

This balance of humility and strength is what makes Hanuman such a powerful and respected figure.

One of the most profound examples of the interplay between humility and strength is the episode where Hanuman allows himself to be captured by Ravana's forces in Lanka. Despite having the strength to defeat them all, Hanuman chooses to surrender, recognizing that his mission is not to destroy but to deliver a message. This act of humility does not make Hanuman weak; rather, it highlights his inner strength and his ability to prioritize the greater good over his own pride. This episode is a powerful reminder that true strength is not just about the ability to fight, but also about the wisdom to know when to exercise restraint.

Hanuman's humility and strength also come together in his role as a leader. Despite being a powerful warrior, Hanuman never seeks to dominate or control others. Instead, he leads by example, inspiring others with his selflessness, courage, and devotion. His humility allows him to connect with others on a deep level, earning their trust and respect. At the same time, his strength gives him the ability to protect and guide them, ensuring that they stay on the path of dharma. This combination of humility and strength makes Hanuman an ideal leader, one who leads not through fear or force, but through love and service.

In many ways, Hanuman's humility and strength are reflections of the divine qualities of Rama. Just as Rama is the epitome of righteousness and compassion, Hanuman embodies the qualities of humility and strength. His devotion to Rama is not just a matter of faith, but also a reflection of his deep understanding of these divine qualities. By aligning himself with Rama, Hanuman is able to manifest these qualities in his own life, becoming a living example of the power of humility and strength.

The Lessons of Hanuman's Humility and Strength: A Guide for Life

Hanuman's unique combination of humility and strength offers valuable lessons for all of us. In a world where power is often equated with dominance and success is measured by personal achievement, Hanuman's example challenges us to rethink our understanding of strength and humility.

One of the key lessons from Hanuman's life is the idea that **true strength comes from humility**. In Hanuman, we see that strength is not about overpowering others or asserting one's superiority, but about using one's abilities for the greater good. This strength is rooted in a deep sense of humility, which allows us to recognize our limitations and to understand that our abilities are gifts to be used in the service of others. Hanuman's example teaches us that when strength is guided by humility, it becomes a force for good, capable of transforming the world.

Another important lesson from Hanuman's life is the **importance of selflessness**. Hanuman's strength is always used in the service of others, never for his own gain. This selflessness is a reflection of his humility, which keeps his ego in check and ensures that his actions are always aligned with the divine will. Hanuman's example reminds us that true greatness lies not in seeking personal glory, but in serving others and fulfilling our higher purpose.

Hanuman's life also teaches us the value of **restraint and discernment**. Despite his immense power, Hanuman does not use his strength recklessly or without purpose. He understands when to fight and when to exercise restraint, and his actions are always guided by a sense of righteousness and justice. This discernment is a key aspect of Hanuman's strength, allowing him to navigate complex situations with wisdom and clarity. Hanuman's example encourages us to develop this same sense of discernment in our own lives, using our strength not just to achieve our goals, but to uphold the principles of dharma.

Finally, Hanuman's life offers a powerful lesson in the **power of devotion**. It is Hanuman's devotion to Rama that gives him the strength to overcome any obstacle and to remain humble in the face of success. This devotion is a reminder that true strength comes from a deep connection with the divine, and that humility is the natural result of recognizing our place in the larger scheme of things. Hanuman's example challenges us to cultivate this same sense of devotion in our own lives, using our strengths and abilities in the service of a higher purpose.

Conclusion: The Eternal Relevance of Hanuman's Humility and Strength

Hanuman's life is a testament to the transformative power of humility and strength. These two qualities, when combined, create a powerful force capable of overcoming any challenge and achieving the highest goals. Hanuman's example is not just a story from ancient mythology, but a timeless guide for living a life of purpose, service, and spiritual growth.

In a world where power is often seen as the ultimate goal, Hanuman's life reminds us that true strength lies in humility. It is through humility that we can recognize our true potential, connect with others, and align ourselves with the divine will. Hanuman's strength, guided by his humility, is a model for how we can use our own abilities to make a positive impact on the world.

As we reflect on Hanuman's life, we are reminded of the importance of balancing strength with humility, power with compassion, and action with wisdom. Hanuman's story encourages us to look beyond our own desires and to dedicate our lives to a higher purpose. In doing so, we can find the strength to overcome our own challenges, the wisdom to navigate the complexities of life, and the peace that comes from living in harmony with our higher purpose.

Hanuman's humility and strength are not just virtues to be admired, but qualities to be cultivated in our own lives. By following Hanuman's example, we can develop the inner strength and humility needed to face life's challenges with courage and grace, and to live a life of service, devotion, and spiritual fulfillment.

CHAPTER V

The Leap to Lanka: Overcoming Impossible Odds

Faith Beyond Fear: Hanuman's Journey Across the Seas and the Power of Determination

The episode of Hanuman's leap to Lanka is one of the most iconic and symbolic moments in the Ramayana, representing the triumph of faith, courage, and determination over seemingly insurmountable obstacles. This event is not merely a tale of physical prowess; it is a profound metaphor for the challenges we face in life and the inner strength required to overcome them. In this chapter, we will explore the detailed narrative of Hanuman's leap, the obstacles he encountered, the symbolic meanings behind these challenges, and the lessons we can draw from this epic journey.

The Context of the Leap: A Mission of Utmost Importance

The leap to Lanka occurs at a critical juncture in the Ramayana. Sita, the beloved wife of Lord Rama, has been abducted by Ravana, the demon king of Lanka. Rama, along with his brother Lakshmana and a devoted army of vanaras (monkey warriors), led by their king Sugriva, embarks on a quest to rescue her. However, despite their best efforts, Sita's exact location remains unknown. It is Hanuman who is tasked with the crucial mission of crossing the vast ocean to Lanka, finding Sita, and delivering Rama's message to her.

This mission is not just important; it is vital for the success of Rama's entire campaign. The stakes are incredibly high, and the task seems almost impossible. The leap to Lanka is not just a test of Hanuman's physical strength but also of his faith, determination, and ability to overcome fear and doubt. It is a journey that will push him to his limits and beyond, challenging every aspect of his being.

The Ocean: A Symbol of Overwhelming Challenges

The first and most obvious obstacle that Hanuman faces is the ocean itself. Spanning hundreds of miles, the ocean represents the vast and seemingly insurmountable challenges that stand between Hanuman and his goal. The ocean is a powerful symbol in Hindu mythology, often representing the unknown, the unconscious mind, and the vastness of the universe. Crossing the ocean is not just a physical act but a metaphorical journey into the depths of the self, where one must confront inner fears, doubts, and limitations.

As Hanuman stands on the shore, contemplating the daunting task ahead of him, he must first overcome his own doubts. Despite his immense strength and divine abilities, the sheer scale of the challenge is enough to give pause to even the mightiest of beings. This moment of hesitation is crucial, as it reflects the universal human experience of facing overwhelming odds. No matter how strong or capable we may be, there are times when the magnitude of the challenges before us can seem too great to overcome.

However, it is in this moment of doubt that Hanuman's true character is revealed. Instead of giving in to fear, Hanuman recalls his divine nature and the blessings of Lord Rama. He draws upon his inner strength and his unwavering devotion to Rama, which empowers him to take the leap. This moment of realization is a powerful reminder that faith and determination can overcome even the most daunting obstacles. The leap to Lanka symbolizes the leap of faith that we all must take at some point in our lives—trusting in our abilities, our purpose, and the divine support that guides us.

The Leap: A Marvel of Physical and Spiritual Strength

The actual leap to Lanka is a feat of incredible physical prowess. Hanuman, who possesses the ability to change his size at will, expands to a colossal form and launches himself into the air with such force that the very earth trembles. As he soars through the sky, Hanuman's leap becomes a testament to the power of self-belief and the strength that comes from aligning oneself with a higher purpose.

However, the leap is not just a display of brute strength. It is also a deeply spiritual act, representing the transcendence of human limitations through divine grace. In this moment, Hanuman is not merely a vanara; he is a divine force, an instrument of Lord Rama's will. His leap is powered not just by his physical strength but by his devotion, faith, and the blessings of the divine. This combination of physical and spiritual strength is what makes Hanuman's leap so extraordinary.

As Hanuman soars over the ocean, he is confronted by various obstacles, each representing a different challenge that must be overcome. These obstacles are not just physical barriers but also symbolic of the inner challenges that we all face on our journey towards our goals. Hanuman's ability to overcome these obstacles is a reflection of his inner strength and his unwavering commitment to his mission.

Mainaka Mountain: The Temptation to Rest and the Power of Focus

The first obstacle that Hanuman encounters during his leap is the Mainaka Mountain. As Hanuman flies over the ocean, the mountain rises from the depths, offering him a place to rest. Mainaka is not an enemy; in fact, the mountain offers Hanuman hospitality, a chance to rest and rejuvenate before continuing his journey. This moment represents the temptation to pause, to take a break, and perhaps even to delay the mission.

Mainaka's offer is a symbol of the distractions and temptations that we all face when pursuing a difficult goal. These distractions may not be inherently bad; they may even be well-meaning, like the mountain's offer to Hanuman. However, they can divert us from our path and delay the achievement of our goals. In this moment, Hanuman must choose between the comfort of rest and the urgency of his mission.

Hanuman's response to Mainaka is a powerful lesson in the importance of focus and determination. Recognizing the good intentions of the mountain, Hanuman politely declines the offer, explaining that he cannot afford to rest until he has completed his mission. He acknowledges the importance of rest but understands that this is not the time for it. This decision highlights Hanuman's ability to prioritize his mission above all else, maintaining his focus and not allowing himself to be swayed by distractions.

This encounter with Mainaka teaches us that while rest and relaxation are important, there are times when we must push forward, even when it is difficult. It is a reminder that in the pursuit of our goals, we must remain focused and not allow ourselves to be sidetracked by temporary comforts or distractions. Hanuman's ability to stay focused on his mission, despite the temptation to rest, is a key aspect of his success and a valuable lesson for anyone facing difficult challenges.

Surasa: The Test of Courage and the Power of Adaptability

As Hanuman continues his journey, he is confronted by Surasa, a powerful demoness who is sent by the gods to test his courage and resolve. Surasa appears before Hanuman and demands that he enter her mouth as a test of his strength. This challenge is not just a physical one but also a test of Hanuman's adaptability and quick thinking.

Surasa represents the unforeseen challenges that arise on our journey, testing our courage and forcing us to think on our feet. These challenges often come without warning and require us to adapt quickly to new circumstances. In this situation, Hanuman must use not just his strength but also his intelligence and cunning to overcome the obstacle.

Rather than fighting Surasa head-on, Hanuman uses his ability to change his size to outwit her. He first grows to an enormous size, challenging Surasa to match him. Then, in a sudden move, he shrinks to the size of a thumb and quickly enters and exits her mouth, fulfilling her demand without being harmed. This clever maneuver allows Hanuman to continue his journey without delay.

The encounter with Surasa teaches us the importance of adaptability and quick thinking when facing challenges. Hanuman's ability to think creatively and use his unique abilities to overcome the obstacle is a powerful reminder that strength alone is not always enough. Sometimes, we must be willing to adapt and find new ways to achieve our goals. Hanuman's success in this challenge is a testament to his resourcefulness and his ability to remain calm and focused under pressure.

Simhika: The Battle with the Shadow and Overcoming Inner Darkness

The next obstacle that Hanuman faces is Simhika, a demoness with the power to grasp the shadow of any being and drag them down to their doom. As Hanuman flies over the ocean, Simhika spots his shadow and seizes it, pulling him down towards the water. This encounter is one of the most dangerous challenges that Hanuman faces, as it represents the power of inner darkness and negativity that can drag us down and prevent us from reaching our goals.

Simhika is a symbol of the inner demons that we all carry—the fears, doubts, and negative emotions that can hold us back and sabotage our efforts. These inner shadows can be incredibly powerful, and they often strike when we are at our most vulnerable. Hanuman's battle with Simhika is a metaphor for the struggle against these inner forces, which must be confronted and overcome if we are to succeed.

In this encounter, Hanuman once again demonstrates his incredible strength and determination. Realizing that he cannot escape Simhika's grasp through flight alone, Hanuman dives down towards the demoness and engages her in combat. Using his immense strength and martial prowess, Hanuman defeats Simhika, tearing her apart and freeing himself from her grasp.

This battle with Simhika is a powerful reminder that we must confront our inner demons head-on if we are to overcome them. It is not enough to simply ignore or avoid these negative forces; we must face them directly and use our inner strength to defeat them. Hanuman's victory over Simhika is a testament to the power of courage and determination in overcoming inner darkness, and it serves as an inspiration to anyone facing similar struggles.

The Arrival in Lanka: The Final Test and the Power of Stealth

After overcoming these formidable obstacles, Hanuman finally arrives in Lanka, the island kingdom of Ravana. However, his challenges are far from over. Lanka is a land filled with dangers, and Hanuman must use all of his skills and abilities to navigate this hostile environment without being detected. This phase of Hanuman's journey represents the final test of his strength, courage, and cunning.

Upon arriving in Lanka, Hanuman is confronted with the towering walls and heavily guarded gates of Ravana's city. The kingdom is a place of darkness and evil, filled with powerful demons and treacherous traps. To succeed in his mission, Hanuman must find a way to enter the city undetected and locate Sita without alerting the enemy to his presence.

This part of Hanuman's journey is a test of his stealth and intelligence. Recognizing the dangers of being discovered, Hanuman shrinks down to a tiny size and carefully makes his way through the city. He moves silently and swiftly, avoiding detection by the numerous guards and sentries. This ability to move unnoticed is a reflection of Hanuman's humility and his understanding of the importance of discretion and caution.

As Hanuman explores the city, he encounters numerous temptations and distractions, but he remains focused on his mission. He resists the allure of wealth and power, maintaining his single-minded devotion to finding Sita and delivering Rama's message. This final test is a testament to Hanuman's unwavering commitment to his mission and his ability to stay true to his purpose despite the many dangers and temptations that surround him.

Finding Sita: The Triumph of Faith and the Fulfillment of the Mission

After navigating the treacherous landscape of Lanka, Hanuman finally locates Sita in the Ashoka Vatika, a beautiful garden where she is being held captive by Ravana. The sight of Sita, sorrowful and in distress, fills Hanuman with both compassion and resolve. He realizes that his mission is not just about finding Sita but also about giving her hope and reassurance.

Hanuman's encounter with Sita is a powerful moment, representing the triumph of faith and devotion. He approaches her with great humility and reverence, recognizing her as the embodiment of purity and devotion. Hanuman delivers Rama's message to Sita, assuring her that Rama is coming to rescue her and that she must remain strong and steadfast in her faith.

This moment of connection between Hanuman and Sita is deeply symbolic. It represents the meeting of the divine and the human, the connection between faith and action. Hanuman's success in finding Sita and delivering Rama's message is the culmination of his journey, a testament to the power of devotion, courage, and determination. It is also a moment of profound spiritual significance, as Hanuman's unwavering faith in Rama is mirrored in Sita's unwavering faith in her husband.

The Return to Rama: A Hero's Welcome and the Lessons of the Leap

After completing his mission in Lanka, Hanuman returns to Rama with the news of Sita's whereabouts. His return journey is swift, fueled by the knowledge that he has succeeded in his mission and that Rama's reunion with Sita is now within reach. Upon his return, Hanuman is greeted as a hero, his courage and devotion celebrated by Rama and the entire vanara army.

Hanuman's successful leap to Lanka and back is more than just a physical feat; it is a journey of spiritual growth and self-realization. Through this journey, Hanuman demonstrates the power of faith, the strength of devotion, and the importance of perseverance in the face of overwhelming odds. His leap to Lanka is a metaphor for the challenges we all face in life, and his ability to overcome these challenges offers valuable lessons for us all.

One of the key lessons from Hanuman's leap to Lanka is the importance of faith and self-belief. Hanuman's journey is a testament to the power of believing in oneself and in the divine support that guides us. Despite the immense challenges he faces, Hanuman never loses faith in his abilities or in the righteousness of his mission. This faith is what allows him to overcome every obstacle and achieve the seemingly impossible.

Another important lesson from Hanuman's journey is the value of perseverance and determination. Hanuman's leap to Lanka is not an easy one; it requires immense strength, courage, and endurance. However, Hanuman never gives up, even when the challenges seem insurmountable. His determination to succeed, no matter what, is a powerful reminder that we too can overcome the obstacles in our own lives if we remain steadfast in our goals.

Hanuman's journey also teaches us the importance of humility and service. Despite his incredible strength and abilities, Hanuman never seeks glory or recognition for himself. His only concern is fulfilling his duty to Rama and serving the greater good. This selflessness is a key aspect of Hanuman's greatness, and it serves as a reminder that true strength lies in service to others.

Finally, Hanuman's leap to Lanka is a testament to the power of devotion. Hanuman's unwavering devotion to Rama is the driving force behind his every action. It is this devotion that gives him the strength to overcome all obstacles and to achieve his goal. Hanuman's example challenges us to cultivate this same sense of devotion in our own lives, using our strengths and abilities in the service of a higher purpose.

In conclusion, Hanuman's leap to Lanka is a powerful and inspiring story of overcoming impossible odds. It is a journey that teaches us valuable lessons about faith, perseverance, humility, and devotion. Through his courage, determination, and unwavering commitment to his mission, Hanuman shows us that no challenge is too great, no obstacle too insurmountable, if we approach it with the right mindset and a heart full of faith. Hanuman's leap to Lanka is not just a story from ancient mythology; it is a timeless guide for facing the challenges of life with courage, strength, and grace.

CHAPTER VI

The Burning of Lanka: Righteous Anger

When Fury is Just: Understanding the Role of Justice in Divine Wrath

The burning of Lanka by Hanuman is one of the most dramatic and significant episodes in the Ramayana. It is an act that encapsulates the complex emotions and moral dilemmas associated with anger, particularly when it is justified or deemed righteous. Through this act, Hanuman demonstrates that anger, when channeled for a righteous cause, can serve as a powerful force for justice. This chapter delves deeply into the events leading up to the burning of Lanka, the symbolic meanings of this act, and the lessons it offers about the nature of righteous anger and its consequences.

The Prelude to Destruction: Hanuman's Mission and Capture

After successfully locating Sita in the Ashoka Vatika and delivering Rama's message, Hanuman faces a critical decision. His mission, as assigned by Rama, was to find Sita, ascertain her safety, and return with this information. However, after conversing with Sita and reassuring her of Rama's imminent arrival, Hanuman realizes that he has an opportunity to do more. His keen strategic mind tells him that he can gather valuable intelligence on Lanka's defenses and assess the strength of Ravana's forces, which would be crucial for Rama's eventual attack.

Driven by this sense of duty, Hanuman begins to explore the city of Lanka. He moves stealthily, observing the various fortifications, the numbers and disposition of Ravana's demon army, and the general layout of the city. His initial reconnaissance is successful, but as he ventures further into the heart of the city, Hanuman's presence is eventually discovered.

The demons of Lanka are initially bewildered by the sight of this strange monkey-like figure moving through their city with such confidence. However, as Hanuman begins to engage them in combat—defeating several demons with ease—his identity as a powerful and potentially divine being becomes apparent. The news of Hanuman's presence quickly reaches Ravana, who orders his capture.

The demons, led by the formidable Indrajit, Ravana's son, manage to capture Hanuman using the Brahmastra, a powerful celestial weapon. Despite being captured, Hanuman's composure remains unshaken. His capture is, in many ways, a deliberate act. Hanuman knows that by allowing himself to be brought before Ravana, he can confront the demon king directly, deliver Rama's message, and perhaps even weaken Ravana's resolve.

The Court of Ravana: Confrontation and the Limits of Diplomacy

Hanuman is brought in chains to Ravana's court, where he is surrounded by the assembled might of Lanka's demon lords. This moment is one of high tension, as it represents a direct confrontation between the forces of good and evil. Ravana, confident in his power and authority, initially underestimates Hanuman, seeing him only as a troublesome messenger. However, Hanuman's bearing, his refusal to be intimidated, and his calm yet defiant words soon make it clear that he is no ordinary being.

In Ravana's court, Hanuman boldly speaks of Rama's virtues and the righteousness of his cause. He delivers Rama's message to Ravana, urging him to return Sita and seek peace, warning him of the dire consequences if he persists in his evil ways. This moment is a critical one, as it highlights the limits of diplomacy when dealing with those who are consumed by ego and malice.

Ravana, rather than heeding Hanuman's warning, is enraged by the audacity of this messenger. The demon king's pride blinds him to the wisdom in Hanuman's words. In his anger, Ravana orders Hanuman's execution. However, Vibhishana, Ravana's righteous brother who would later defect to Rama's side, intervenes. He points out that killing a messenger is against the codes of dharma, even in war. Reluctantly, Ravana agrees but decides to humiliate Hanuman instead by setting his tail on fire—a punishment he believes will break Hanuman's spirit and send a clear message to Rama and his allies.

The Burning Tail: Transformation of Anger into Action

As the demons bind Hanuman's tail in cloth and soak it in oil, preparing to set it alight, Hanuman remains calm. He recognizes that this act of humiliation is more than just an attack on his person; it is an affront to his mission, to Rama, and to the very principles of dharma. This realization triggers a transformation within Hanuman—his righteous anger begins to surface.

When Hanuman's tail is finally set on fire, instead of succumbing to the pain or the intended humiliation, Hanuman taps into his divine powers. He begins to grow in size, breaking free of his bonds. With his tail ablaze, Hanuman leaps from building to building, using the very fire that was meant to punish him as a weapon against the city of Lanka.

This act of setting Lanka on fire is not a random act of destruction but a calculated response to the evil that Ravana's kingdom represents. The flames that Hanuman spreads through the city are symbolic of the purifying power of righteous anger. Just as fire burns away impurities, Hanuman's act is meant to cleanse Lanka of its evil, to deliver a warning to Ravana, and to demonstrate the futility of opposing the forces of dharma.

The Destruction of Lanka: The Consequences of Righteous Anger

As Hanuman moves through Lanka, the flames from his tail spread rapidly, engulfing homes, palaces, and fortifications. The once-mighty city, a symbol of Ravana's power and hubris, begins to crumble under the onslaught of the fire. Hanuman's leap from building to building, setting each alight, is a vivid image of the power of righteous anger when it is unleashed for a just cause.

The burning of Lanka serves multiple purposes. On a practical level, it weakens Ravana's defenses and demoralizes his forces, giving Rama a significant advantage in the forthcoming battle. However, the act is also deeply symbolic. The destruction of Lanka represents the inevitable downfall of evil when it is confronted by the forces of righteousness. Ravana's kingdom, built on a foundation of adharma (unrighteousness), is shown to be vulnerable, despite its outward appearance of strength.

Hanuman's act of burning Lanka is also a reminder of the consequences of unchecked pride and arrogance. Ravana's refusal to heed the warnings of Rama's messenger, his disdain for the codes of dharma, and his overconfidence in his own power lead directly to this destruction. In this sense, the burning of Lanka is not just an act of retribution but also a form of divine justice. It is a demonstration that those who act against dharma will ultimately face the consequences of their actions.

The scene of Lanka burning is both terrifying and awe-inspiring. The city, which had once been a place of grandeur, is reduced to ashes in a matter of hours. The flames reflect the intensity of Hanuman's righteous anger, an anger that is not born of hatred or revenge but of a deep commitment to justice and dharma. The destruction is comprehensive, affecting both the high and the low, the rich and the poor, symbolizing that adharma spares no one when it is met with divine retribution.

The Aftermath: Reflection on Anger and Its Power

After the city has been thoroughly ravaged by fire, Hanuman's anger subsides. He returns to his normal size and extinguishes the flames on his tail by dipping it into the ocean. This act of cooling down represents the return of Hanuman's calm and composed nature after his righteous anger has served its purpose. The shift from destructive force back to peaceful service highlights the duality of Hanuman's character—his ability to be both a fierce warrior and a humble devotee.

In the aftermath of the burning, Lanka lies in ruins, and the demons are left in shock and despair. Ravana, for all his might, has been given a glimpse of the power he is up against. However, rather than being cowed, Ravana's pride and anger only deepen, setting the stage for the eventual great battle between good and evil.

For Hanuman, the burning of Lanka is not an act of personal revenge but a necessary step in fulfilling his duty to Rama and upholding dharma. He does not take pleasure in the destruction; instead, he sees it as a means to an end—a way to weaken Ravana and bring about the eventual liberation of Sita and the restoration of righteousness.

This episode prompts reflection on the nature of anger and its role in human life. Anger is often seen as a negative emotion, one that can lead to destructive and harmful behavior. However, in the context of Hanuman's actions, anger is shown to have a place in the moral order when it is controlled, focused, and used for a just cause. This is what differentiates righteous anger from the destructive anger born of ego, hatred, or malice.

Hanuman's anger is rooted in his deep sense of justice and his commitment to dharma. It is an anger that arises in response to the violation of moral principles, to the suffering of the innocent, and to the arrogance of those who believe they are above divine law. This form of anger, when expressed in a controlled and purposeful manner, becomes a force for good. It is a reminder that not all anger is to be suppressed; there are times when it is necessary to stand up, to fight, and to destroy that which is evil and unjust.

Lessons from the Burning of Lanka: The Dual Nature of Anger

The burning of Lanka offers several profound lessons on the dual nature of anger and its potential both to destroy and to purify. Hanuman's actions teach us that anger, in itself, is not inherently bad; it is the context, motivation, and control of that anger that determine its moral value.

Anger as a Response to Injustice: Hanuman's anger is triggered by the injustice he witnesses—Sita's abduction, Ravana's defiance of dharma, and the suffering of the people under his rule. This anger is not a reaction to personal affronts but a response to the violation of moral and ethical principles. It is this sense of righteous indignation that drives Hanuman to act, transforming his anger into a force for justice.

The Importance of Control and Purpose: While Hanuman's anger leads to the destruction of Lanka, it is carefully controlled and directed. Hanuman does not allow his anger to overwhelm him or to lead to senseless destruction. Instead, he channels it with precision, using it to weaken Ravana's power while avoiding unnecessary harm to the innocent. This demonstrates the importance of controlling one's anger and using it in a way that serves a higher purpose.

The Transitory Nature of Anger: After the burning of Lanka, Hanuman's anger dissipates, and he returns to his peaceful and composed state. This highlights the idea that anger, even when righteous, should not be a permanent state of being. Once it has served its purpose, it should be let go, allowing for the return of calm and rational thought. This ability to move beyond anger is what distinguishes Hanuman and makes him a model of self-control and wisdom.

The Consequences of Righteous Anger: The burning of Lanka is a clear demonstration of the consequences that can arise when righteous anger is unleashed. While it serves the purpose of justice, it also brings about significant destruction. This serves as a reminder that even righteous actions can have far-reaching consequences, and one must be prepared to face them. It also underscores the importance of using anger as a last resort, when all other avenues for justice have been exhausted.

The Role of Anger in the Moral Order: Finally, Hanuman's actions remind us that anger has a place within the moral order of the universe. While often viewed negatively, anger, when aligned with dharma and expressed in service of justice, becomes a necessary force for maintaining balance and order. Hanuman's burning of Lanka is not an act of chaos but one of retribution and purification, aimed at restoring the moral balance disrupted by Ravana's actions.

Conclusion: The Burning of Lanka as a Symbol of Justice

The burning of Lanka by Hanuman stands as one of the most powerful symbols of justice in the Ramayana. It is an act that challenges our understanding of anger, showing us that when anger is rooted in righteousness, it can become a potent force for good. Hanuman's actions serve as a reminder that there are times when we must rise up against injustice, even if it means engaging in acts of destruction to bring about a greater good.

Hanuman's burning of Lanka is not just a physical act of setting a city ablaze; it is a spiritual act of purging evil, a manifestation of divine justice. It teaches us that while anger can be dangerous and destructive, it can also be purifying and redemptive when it is controlled and directed towards upholding dharma.

The lessons from this episode extend far beyond the boundaries of the Ramayana, offering timeless wisdom on the nature of anger, justice, and the moral complexities of human action. In Hanuman's story, we find a guide to understanding how to channel our emotions, particularly anger, in ways that align with our highest values and contribute to the greater good.

As we reflect on the burning of Lanka, we are reminded of the importance of righteousness, the power of controlled anger, and the need to act with both strength and compassion in the face of evil. Hanuman's example challenges us to look within ourselves, to recognize the potential for both destruction and creation in our emotions, and to strive always to use that power in the service of justice, truth, and dharma.

CHAPTER VII

The Sanjeevani Mission: Timeliness and Decision Making

Racing Against Time: The Art of Quick Thinking and Strategic Decisions

The Sanjeevani mission undertaken by Hanuman during the Ramayana is a tale of extraordinary courage, urgency, and decisive action. This episode, rich in symbolism and moral teachings, showcases the critical importance of timely decision-making, the value of resourcefulness, and the weight of responsibility when lives hang in the balance. Through Hanuman's mission to retrieve the Sanjeevani herb, the narrative imparts profound lessons on the essence of leadership, the nature of faith, and the power of determination. In this chapter, we will explore the circumstances leading up to the Sanjeevani mission, the challenges Hanuman faced, the decisions he made, and the broader implications of this iconic episode.

The Wounded Lakshmana: A Crisis Unfolds

The Sanjeevani mission occurs during one of the most intense and critical phases of the battle between Rama's forces and Ravana's army in Lanka. The war has reached a fever pitch, with both sides suffering heavy casualties. The vanaras, under the command of Rama and Lakshmana, have fought valiantly against the demon horde, but the battle is far from over. It is in this chaotic and perilous environment that Lakshmana, Rama's devoted brother and closest companion, is grievously wounded.

Lakshmana's injury is not just a physical blow; it represents a critical turning point in the battle. As the beloved younger brother of Rama and a key warrior in the fight against Ravana, Lakshmana's fall sends shockwaves through the ranks of the vanaras. His injury occurs at the hands of Indrajit, Ravana's son, who is renowned for his prowess in battle and his mastery of powerful weapons. Indrajit strikes Lakshmana with the Shakti weapon, a celestial spear that renders Lakshmana unconscious and on the brink of death.

The sight of Lakshmana lying lifeless on the battlefield is a moment of profound despair for Rama. Despite his divine nature, Rama is overcome with grief at the thought of losing his brother. This moment of vulnerability adds a human dimension to Rama's character, highlighting the deep bond of love and loyalty that exists between the two brothers. For Rama, Lakshmana is more than just a sibling; he is a reflection of his own soul, his constant companion in exile, and his unwavering support in every trial.

As the gravity of the situation becomes clear, the vanaras, who had looked to Lakshmana as a pillar of strength, begin to falter. The morale of the army, already strained by the long and brutal conflict, is further weakened by the sight of their beloved leader lying mortally wounded. The battlefield, once a place of determined struggle, now feels like the setting of inevitable defeat.

The Search for a Cure: A Race Against Time

Amidst this atmosphere of despair, Sushena, the vanara physician, is called upon to examine Lakshmana. Sushena, wise and knowledgeable in the healing arts, quickly assesses the severity of the wound. He determines that Lakshmana's only hope for survival lies in a rare and powerful herb known as Sanjeevani. This miraculous herb, famed for its ability to restore life, grows only on the sacred mountain Dronagiri (also known as Gandhamadana), far to the north in the Himalayas.

The challenge of obtaining the Sanjeevani herb is immense. Not only is the mountain where it grows located a great distance from the battlefield, but the journey to retrieve it is fraught with peril. The herb must be brought back before the dawn of the next day, or it will be too late to save Lakshmana. This sets the stage for one of the most urgent and heroic missions in the Ramayana—one that requires extraordinary speed, strength, and decision-making.

The responsibility of fetching the Sanjeevani falls to Hanuman, the only one among Rama's forces capable of undertaking such a daunting task. Hanuman's strength, speed, and divine abilities make him the ideal candidate for this mission, but even for him, the challenge is formidable. The distance to Dronagiri is vast, and time is of the essence. Every moment lost brings Lakshmana closer to death, and with him, the hopes of Rama and the vanara army.

Hanuman, recognizing the urgency of the situation, does not hesitate. His sense of duty, loyalty to Rama, and love for Lakshmana propel him into immediate action. Without delay, Hanuman assumes his immense form and takes to the skies, beginning the perilous journey to the Himalayas. This moment marks the beginning of a race against time—a mission where success means life, and failure means death.

The Flight to the Himalayas: Overcoming Obstacles

As Hanuman flies across the skies, covering vast distances with each leap, he encounters several obstacles that test his resolve and abilities. The journey to the Himalayas is not just a physical test but also a spiritual and mental one. Hanuman's unwavering focus on his mission is what enables him to overcome these challenges, each of which carries symbolic significance.

One of the first obstacles Hanuman faces is the mountain of Mainaka, which rises from the ocean to offer him rest. Mainaka, a friend of Hanuman's father, Vayu, seeks to provide Hanuman with a place to rest and refresh himself. However, Hanuman, understanding the urgency of his mission, politely declines the offer, explaining that he cannot afford to waste even a single moment. This encounter illustrates Hanuman's deep sense of responsibility and his ability to prioritize his duties over personal comfort.

As Hanuman continues his journey, he is confronted by Surasa, the mother of serpents, who has been sent by the gods to test his determination. Surasa demands that Hanuman enter her mouth before continuing on his way. Hanuman, recognizing this as a divine test, uses his wit and agility to outmaneuver her. He shrinks to a tiny size, enters Surasa's mouth, and exits instantly, fulfilling her demand without being delayed. This episode highlights Hanuman's quick thinking and his ability to adapt to challenges without losing focus on his goal.

Another significant challenge comes from Simhika, a demoness who has the power to capture beings by grasping their shadows. As Hanuman's shadow passes over her, Simhika seizes it, pulling him down towards the ocean. Hanuman, realizing the danger, swiftly grows in size and defeats Simhika with a single blow. This confrontation symbolizes the internal and external forces that seek to pull one down in moments of crisis, and Hanuman's victory represents the triumph of determination and courage over such obstacles.

These encounters during Hanuman's flight to the Himalayas are not just physical barriers; they represent the various forms of distraction, temptation, and opposition that one may face when undertaking a critical task. Hanuman's ability to overcome each of these obstacles without losing sight of his mission underscores his exemplary decision-making skills and his unwavering commitment to his duty.

The Dilemma at Dronagiri: A Critical Decision

Upon reaching the Dronagiri mountain, Hanuman faces the most challenging part of his mission—the task of identifying the Sanjeevani herb. The mountain is home to a variety of herbs, each with its own unique properties, and the Sanjeevani is known to be difficult to distinguish from others. As Hanuman searches the mountain, he realizes that time is slipping away. The urgency of Lakshmana's condition weighs heavily on his mind, and he knows that any further delay could mean the difference between life and death.

Faced with this critical dilemma, Hanuman makes a bold and decisive choice. Rather than risking the possibility of selecting the wrong herb or wasting precious time trying to identify the Sanjeevani, Hanuman decides to uproot the entire mountain and carry it back to Lanka. This decision, though extreme, reflects Hanuman's ability to think creatively under pressure and to make swift decisions in the face of uncertainty.

Hanuman's choice to carry the mountain is a testament to his resourcefulness and his commitment to the mission. It also symbolizes the idea that when the stakes are high, sometimes unconventional and bold actions are necessary to achieve the desired outcome. By choosing to bring the entire mountain, Hanuman ensures that Sushena will have access to the Sanjeevani herb, regardless of any potential errors in identification. This act of carrying the mountain is not only a demonstration of Hanuman's immense physical strength but also of his mental agility and decisiveness.

The Return to Lanka: Delivering the Cure

With the mountain securely in his grasp, Hanuman once again takes to the skies, flying at incredible speed back to the battlefield in Lanka. His return journey is marked by a renewed sense of urgency, as the sun begins to rise, signaling the approach of the deadline for saving Lakshmana. The sight of Hanuman returning with the mountain fills the vanaras and Rama with a renewed sense of hope. It is a moment of triumph, but one that is tempered by the knowledge that time is still of the essence.

As Hanuman arrives back in Lanka, he carefully places the mountain near Sushena, who immediately begins the search for the Sanjeevani herb. The tension in the air is palpable as Sushena works quickly to prepare the remedy that will save Lakshmana's life. The vanara army, along with Rama, watches anxiously, aware that the outcome of this moment will determine the fate of the battle and perhaps the entire war.

Finally, Sushena administers the Sanjeevani to Lakshmana, and miraculously, the young prince begins to stir. The life-giving herb works its magic, reviving Lakshmana from the brink of death. The collective sigh of relief from the vanaras and the joyful tears in Rama's eyes reflect the deep emotional impact of this moment. Lakshmana's recovery not only saves his life but also restores the morale of the vanara army, giving them the strength to continue the fight against Ravana.

Lessons in Timeliness and Decision-Making

The Sanjeevani mission is more than just an episode of physical heroism; it is a profound lesson in the importance of timeliness and decision-making. Hanuman's actions throughout this mission illustrate the qualities of a true leader—one who can remain calm under pressure, think creatively in the face of challenges, and make decisions with confidence, even when the path is uncertain.

One of the key lessons from this episode is the importance of acting with urgency when the situation demands it. Hanuman understands that in the face of life-threatening danger, there is no time to hesitate or to be paralyzed by doubt. His swift action in flying to the Himalayas, his decisive choice to carry the entire mountain, and his rapid return to Lanka all demonstrate the critical importance of timeliness. In situations where lives are at stake, every moment counts, and the ability to act quickly and effectively can make all the difference.

Another important lesson is the value of resourcefulness and creative problem-solving. Hanuman's decision to uproot the mountain rather than risking the selection of the wrong herb shows his ability to think outside the box. In moments of crisis, traditional methods and approaches may not always be sufficient. Hanuman's willingness to take an unconventional route—literally lifting an entire mountain to ensure the success of his mission—illustrates the power of innovative thinking in overcoming seemingly insurmountable obstacles.

Moreover, Hanuman's actions during the Sanjeevani mission highlight the importance of responsibility and the weight of leadership. Hanuman is acutely aware of the responsibility he carries, not only to Lakshmana and Rama but to the entire vanara army and the greater cause they are fighting for. This sense of responsibility drives him to go above and beyond, to push his limits, and to ensure that he fulfills his duty, no matter the personal cost.

The Symbolism of the Sanjeevani Mission

The Sanjeevani mission is rich with symbolism, offering deeper insights into the nature of life, death, and the struggle between good and evil. The Sanjeevani herb itself symbolizes life and hope, a beacon of divine intervention in a world fraught with suffering and mortality. Its life-giving properties serve as a reminder that even in the darkest moments, there is always the potential for renewal and recovery.

Hanuman's journey to obtain the Sanjeevani can also be seen as a metaphor for the spiritual quest for enlightenment and salvation. The mountains, representing obstacles and challenges, must be overcome in order to attain the ultimate goal. Hanuman's successful retrieval of the Sanjeevani symbolizes the triumph of the soul over the difficulties and distractions of the material world, ultimately leading to the preservation of life and the continuation of the righteous path.

The image of Hanuman carrying the mountain on his journey back to Lanka is one of the most iconic in the Ramayana. It represents not only physical strength but also the weight of responsibility and the burden of leadership. Hanuman's act of lifting the mountain is symbolic of the challenges that leaders must bear, the heavy decisions they must make, and the immense pressure that comes with the role of protector and savior.

The Sanjeevani Mission in Contemporary Context

The lessons from Hanuman's Sanjeevani mission are timeless and can be applied to various aspects of contemporary life. In today's fast-paced world, the importance of timely decision-making cannot be overstated. Whether in the realm of business, healthcare, or personal relationships, the ability to make quick, informed decisions is crucial to success and well-being.

Hanuman's resourcefulness and creative problem-solving offer valuable insights for modern leaders and innovators. In a rapidly changing world, traditional solutions may not always be effective, and the ability to think creatively and adapt to new challenges is essential. Hanuman's example encourages us to embrace unconventional approaches when necessary and to be bold in our decision-making.

The Sanjeevani mission also serves as a powerful reminder of the importance of responsibility and ethical leadership. Just as Hanuman carried the weight of the mountain to save Lakshmana's life, contemporary leaders must recognize the impact of their decisions on the lives of others. This sense of responsibility should guide their actions, ensuring that their decisions are made with integrity, compassion, and a commitment to the greater good.

Conclusion: The Legacy of the Sanjeevani Mission

The Sanjeevani mission stands as one of the most dramatic and inspiring episodes in the Ramayana, embodying the qualities of courage, decisiveness, and unwavering commitment to duty. Hanuman's journey to the Himalayas and his triumphant return with the life-saving herb is a story that resonates across cultures and generations, offering timeless lessons on the power of timely action, the value of creative problem-solving, and the responsibilities of leadership.

Through this episode, Hanuman emerges not only as a hero of physical strength but as a symbol of moral and spiritual fortitude. His actions during the Sanjeevani mission exemplify the highest ideals of dharma—acting with urgency and purpose, making decisions with clarity and confidence, and always prioritizing the well-being of others. Hanuman's legacy as a leader, protector, and savior is cemented through this mission, and his example continues to inspire those who seek to navigate the challenges of life with courage, wisdom, and compassion.

In reflecting on the Sanjeevani mission, we are reminded that in the face of impossible odds, it is our ability to act decisively, think creatively, and uphold our responsibilities that ultimately determines our success. Hanuman's story challenges us to rise to the occasion, to embrace the weight of our duties, and to strive always to act in service of life, justice, and the greater good.

CHAPTER VIII

Hanuman's Wisdom and Diplomacy

More Than Muscle: The Influence of Wisdom and Diplomacy in Achieving Success

The character of Hanuman in the Ramayana is often celebrated for his incredible physical strength, unwavering loyalty, and extraordinary devotion. However, these attributes are only part of what makes Hanuman such a revered figure. In addition to his physical prowess, Hanuman also possesses immense wisdom, sharp intellect, and diplomatic acumen. These qualities are vital in many of the key moments in the Ramayana, where brute strength alone would not have sufficed. Through Hanuman's wisdom and diplomacy, we see a nuanced and multi-dimensional hero who is as much a strategist as he is a warrior. This chapter delves deeply into the various instances in the Ramayana where Hanuman's wisdom and diplomatic skills are on full display, examining how they contribute to the overall narrative and what they teach us about effective leadership, the power of communication, and the importance of intellect in navigating complex situations.

The Foundations of Hanuman's Wisdom

Hanuman's wisdom is not a result of mere experience or circumstance; it is deeply rooted in his upbringing and divine heritage. Born to Anjana, a celestial nymph, and Kesari, a mighty vanara chieftain, Hanuman's lineage is one of strength, virtue, and intelligence. However, it is his connection to Vayu, the wind god, who is considered his spiritual father, that imbues Hanuman with a divine spark of knowledge and wisdom.

From a young age, Hanuman is blessed with a curious and inquisitive nature. His early education is comprehensive, covering a wide range of subjects, from the Vedas and scriptures to the arts of war and diplomacy. This broad education is complemented by his close association with learned sages and gods, who impart to him the deeper philosophies of life, dharma, and the intricate balance of cosmic order.

One of the most significant influences on Hanuman's intellectual development is his connection to Surya, the sun god. It is said that Hanuman, in his quest for knowledge, approached Surya to be his teacher. Although Surya initially hesitated, recognizing Hanuman's determination and eagerness to learn, he agreed. Surya imparted to Hanuman the knowledge of the scriptures, science, and various other disciplines. Hanuman's ability to learn while Surya continued his journey across the sky—a feat that required Hanuman to keep pace with the sun's movement—demonstrates not only his physical endurance but also his unparalleled dedication to acquiring wisdom.

This early training, combined with his natural abilities, shapes Hanuman into a being of immense intellect and profound understanding. His wisdom is not merely academic; it is practical, deeply intuitive, and always aligned with dharma, the cosmic law that governs righteousness and justice.

Wisdom in Service of Dharma

Hanuman's wisdom is always in service of a higher purpose. Throughout the Ramayana, his intelligence and strategic thinking are consistently applied in the service of dharma. Whether he is advising Rama, navigating complex situations with Ravana, or outmaneuvering his enemies, Hanuman's actions are guided by a deep understanding of what is just and righteous.

One of the most compelling examples of Hanuman's wisdom in action is his mission to Lanka. Sent by Rama to locate Sita, who has been abducted by Ravana, Hanuman must navigate a perilous journey to the enemy's stronghold. This mission requires more than just physical strength; it demands acute awareness, stealth, and the ability to read situations with precision.

When Hanuman finally locates Sita in the Ashoka Vatika, he does not rush into action. Instead, he carefully observes her from a distance, assessing her emotional state and the environment around her. This shows his understanding of human emotions and his ability to gauge the right moment to reveal himself. Hanuman recognizes that Sita, in her sorrowful state, might not easily trust a stranger appearing out of nowhere, especially in an enemy territory.

To establish trust, Hanuman chooses his words carefully, introducing himself as a devotee of Rama and presenting Rama's ring as proof of his identity. This small but significant gesture instantly reassures Sita, confirming that Hanuman is indeed an ally sent by her beloved husband. Hanuman's approach here is a masterclass in diplomacy—he uses symbols of trust and familiarity to build rapport, ensuring that his message is received with the intended effect.

Furthermore, Hanuman's decision to allow Sita to share her sorrow and speak of her situation before offering solutions is another testament to his wisdom. He understands that in her vulnerable state, Sita needs to express her grief and fears. By listening attentively, Hanuman not only gains valuable information about Ravana's plans but also strengthens the emotional bond between himself and Sita. This bond is crucial for the success of his mission, as it gives Sita hope and strengthens her resolve to endure her captivity until Rama arrives.

Diplomacy in the Heart of the Enemy's Lair

Hanuman's diplomatic skills are further put to the test when he is captured by Ravana's forces after setting Lanka ablaze. Despite being in the heart of the enemy's territory and surrounded by hostile forces, Hanuman remains calm and composed. His capture is not a sign of defeat but an opportunity—an opportunity to deliver a message directly to Ravana and to gauge the demon king's strengths and weaknesses.

When brought before Ravana, Hanuman's approach is one of calculated diplomacy. He does not display fear or submissiveness, nor does he provoke Ravana unnecessarily. Instead, Hanuman speaks with confidence and clarity, delivering Rama's message with the dignity befitting a royal envoy. He uses this moment to not only assert Rama's claim to righteousness but also to offer Ravana a way out—a chance to avoid total destruction by returning Sita and seeking reconciliation.

This encounter is significant because it shows Hanuman's ability to balance firmness with diplomacy. He does not shy away from telling Ravana the harsh truth—that his actions are leading him towards inevitable ruin. Yet, he also offers Ravana a path to redemption, demonstrating his understanding that true diplomacy involves providing solutions, not just pointing out problems.

Moreover, Hanuman's calm demeanor and articulate speech in the face of Ravana's wrath reveal his deep understanding of power dynamics. He knows that his strength lies not in physical combat in this situation, but in the power of words and the righteousness of his cause. His confidence comes from his unwavering belief in dharma, and this unshakable moral foundation allows him to speak truth to power without fear.

This moment also highlights a critical aspect of Hanuman's wisdom—his ability to recognize the right time for diplomacy and the right time for action. When diplomacy fails, as it does with Ravana who dismisses Hanuman's message, Hanuman is prepared to shift tactics. The burning of Lanka is not just an act of revenge; it is a strategic move to demonstrate the power of Rama's forces and to weaken the morale of Ravana's army.

The Power of Persuasion: Hanuman's Role as a Counselor

Throughout the Ramayana, Hanuman's wisdom is not only evident in his actions but also in his role as a counselor to Rama and others. His advice is always rooted in a deep understanding of the situation and the larger cosmic order. One of the most profound instances of Hanuman's counsel occurs during the search for Sita, when the vanara forces, exhausted and demoralized, are on the verge of giving up.

At this critical juncture, Hanuman steps forward to inspire the troops. He reminds them of their duty, the importance of their mission, and the need to persevere despite the difficulties they face. Hanuman's words are not empty rhetoric; they are infused with genuine conviction and a deep understanding of the stakes involved. His ability to inspire and motivate others is a testament to his leadership qualities and his profound wisdom.

Hanuman's counsel is also invaluable to Rama. In many instances, Rama, despite his divine nature, faces moments of doubt and despair, particularly when he is separated from Sita or when the battle against Ravana seems overwhelming. Hanuman's unwavering faith in Rama's mission and his ability to offer perspective during these challenging times make him an indispensable advisor.

For example, when Rama grieves over the prospect of losing Sita forever, it is Hanuman who reassures him, reminding Rama of his own strength, the support of his allies, and the righteousness of his cause. Hanuman's words serve as a balm to Rama's wounded spirit, helping him to regain his composure and focus on the task ahead. This dynamic illustrates the importance of wise counsel in leadership and the value of having trusted advisors who can offer clarity and encouragement in times of crisis.

In addition to advising Rama, Hanuman also plays a key role in negotiating alliances and managing the complex relationships between the various factions that make up Rama's army. His diplomatic skills are crucial in maintaining the unity and morale of the vanaras, as well as in forging alliances with other forces such as the bear king Jambavan and the rakshasa prince Vibhishana, Ravana's own brother, who ultimately defects to Rama's side.

Hanuman's role as a counselor extends beyond mere strategy and tactics; it involves guiding others in understanding and adhering to dharma. His advice is always grounded in the principles of righteousness, justice, and the greater good. This alignment with dharma is what gives Hanuman's words their power and influence, making him not just a warrior and diplomat, but a spiritual guide and moral compass for those around him.

Hanuman's Encounter with Vibhishana: Diplomacy and Moral Conviction

One of the most significant examples of Hanuman's wisdom and diplomacy is his encounter with Vibhishana, Ravana's brother. This episode is a masterclass in the art of negotiation, where Hanuman's ability to assess character and make strategic decisions has far-reaching consequences for the outcome of the war.

Vibhishana, disillusioned by Ravana's unrighteous ways, seeks refuge with Rama. However, his arrival at Rama's camp is met with suspicion and uncertainty by the vanaras, who are wary of a potential spy in their midst. It is Hanuman who steps forward to engage with Vibhishana, carefully assessing his intentions and character.

Hanuman's approach to Vibhishana is marked by caution, but also by a willingness to listen and understand. He does not rush to judgment, but instead, engages in a dialogue that allows Vibhishana to express his grievances and his reasons for abandoning Ravana. Through this conversation, Hanuman discerns Vibhishana's sincerity and his genuine desire to support the cause of righteousness.

Hanuman's decision to support Vibhishana's plea for asylum is a turning point in the narrative. It demonstrates his ability to see beyond surface appearances and to make judgments based on moral conviction rather than fear or prejudice. Hanuman recognizes that Vibhishana's defection is not only a strategic advantage but also a moral victory, as it signifies the triumph of dharma over adharma, even within Ravana's own family.

When Hanuman presents Vibhishana's case to Rama, he does so with thoughtful reasoning. He emphasizes the importance of rewarding those who choose the path of righteousness, regardless of their past associations. Hanuman's counsel in this instance is pivotal in Rama's decision to accept Vibhishana into their fold, a decision that ultimately strengthens their position in the battle against Ravana.

This episode highlights the complex nature of diplomacy, where decisions must be made not only on the basis of immediate benefits but also with an eye towards long-term moral implications. Hanuman's ability to navigate these complexities with wisdom and ethical clarity underscores his role as a diplomat and advisor of the highest order.

The Diplomatic Balancing Act: Hanuman's Role in the War Strategy

As the war between Rama and Ravana progresses, Hanuman's wisdom and diplomacy continue to play a crucial role in shaping the strategies that lead to ultimate victory. Hanuman's role is not confined to the battlefield; he is actively involved in the planning and execution of war strategies that require not only physical might but also psychological insight and careful negotiation.

One of the key moments where Hanuman's diplomatic skills are evident is during the construction of the bridge to Lanka. The challenge of crossing the vast ocean requires not only engineering prowess but also the cooperation of the natural elements and the various beings that inhabit the region. Hanuman's ability to communicate and negotiate with the ocean god and the various forces of nature is instrumental in securing the necessary support for this monumental task.

Hanuman's diplomacy extends to his interactions with the other leaders of Rama's army. He must constantly balance the various interests and temperaments of the vanaras, bears, and other allies, ensuring that their collective efforts remain focused on the common goal. This requires a deep understanding of group dynamics, the ability to mediate conflicts, and the skill to inspire unity among diverse factions.

Throughout the war, Hanuman's counsel is sought on matters ranging from battle tactics to morale-boosting. His insights into Ravana's psychology and his ability to anticipate the enemy's moves are invaluable in outmaneuvering the formidable forces of Lanka. Hanuman's strategic thinking is always informed by his deep knowledge of dharma, ensuring that their actions remain just and righteous, even in the heat of battle.

Hanuman's Legacy as a Diplomat and Wise Counselor

Hanuman's wisdom and diplomacy leave a lasting legacy in the Ramayana, influencing not only the outcome of the war but also the moral lessons that emerge from the epic. His actions demonstrate that true strength is not just physical but also intellectual and moral. Hanuman's ability to navigate complex situations with wisdom, to offer counsel that is both strategic and ethical, and to engage in diplomacy that respects the principles of dharma makes him a role model for leaders and diplomats alike.

In contemporary terms, Hanuman's approach to diplomacy offers valuable lessons for navigating the complexities of modern life. His emphasis on understanding others, his willingness to engage in dialogue, and his commitment to righteousness over expediency are principles that can be applied in various contexts, from international relations to personal relationships.

Moreover, Hanuman's legacy as a wise counselor highlights the importance of having advisors who are not only knowledgeable but also deeply ethical. In a world where decisions are often driven by short-term gains or political expediency, Hanuman's example reminds us of the value of wisdom that is grounded in moral conviction and a long-term vision for the greater good.

Hanuman's wisdom and diplomacy are also a testament to the power of intellect in achieving success. While physical strength and bravery are important, it is Hanuman's sharp mind and strategic thinking that often turn the tide in favor of Rama's forces. His ability to assess situations, make informed decisions, and communicate effectively are qualities that are as crucial today as they were in the ancient world.

In conclusion, Hanuman's wisdom and diplomacy are integral aspects of his character that elevate him from being just a heroic warrior to a figure of profound intellectual and moral significance. Through his actions, Hanuman teaches us that true leadership involves not only courage and strength but also wisdom, foresight, and a deep commitment to justice. His legacy as a diplomat and wise counselor continues to inspire, offering timeless lessons on the power of wisdom in the pursuit of righteousness and the importance of diplomacy in navigating the complexities of life.

CHAPTER IX

Loyalty and Selflessness

Sacrifices for the Greater Good: Lessons in True Devotion and Dedication

Loyalty and selflessness are two of the most defining characteristics of Hanuman, the mighty hero of the Ramayana. These traits are deeply embedded in every action, every decision, and every thought that Hanuman exhibits throughout the epic. Hanuman's unwavering loyalty to Lord Rama and his boundless selflessness elevate him from being just a powerful warrior to a divine figure revered for his virtue and devotion. In this chapter, we delve into the profound depths of Hanuman's loyalty and selflessness, exploring how these qualities define his character, influence the course of events in the Ramayana, and offer timeless lessons for humanity.

The Essence of Loyalty: Hanuman's Unyielding Devotion to Lord Rama

Loyalty, in its truest sense, is the steadfast allegiance to a cause, a person, or a principle, regardless of the challenges and temptations that may arise. In Hanuman, this loyalty is personified in his unwavering devotion to Lord Rama. From the moment Hanuman meets Rama, his life finds its ultimate purpose—serving and protecting Rama in every possible way. This loyalty is not just a sense of duty but a deep spiritual bond that transcends the material world.

Hanuman's loyalty to Rama is first and foremost a reflection of his recognition of Rama's divinity. Unlike many others who see Rama as a mere prince or a powerful warrior, Hanuman perceives

Rama as the incarnation of Vishnu, the preserver of the universe. This recognition is not merely intellectual but an intuitive, heartfelt understanding that guides Hanuman's every action. Hanuman's loyalty is thus rooted in his spiritual insight, which allows him to see beyond the mundane and recognize the divine mission that Rama embodies.

One of the most powerful demonstrations of Hanuman's loyalty is his tireless effort to find Sita after her abduction by Ravana. This mission is not just an act of service; it is a testament to Hanuman's unwavering commitment to Rama's cause. Hanuman embarks on this perilous journey not for personal glory or reward, but purely out of his devotion to Rama. The challenges he faces along the way—crossing the ocean, battling demons, and infiltrating Lanka—are met with courage and determination, driven by his singular focus on fulfilling Rama's wishes.

Hanuman's loyalty is also evident in the way he consistently prioritizes Rama's needs above his own. When Hanuman finds Sita in the Ashoka Vatika, his first thought is not of his own accomplishment but of how to reassure Sita and convey Rama's message to her. Even in moments of triumph, Hanuman remains humble, attributing all success to Rama's grace rather than his own abilities. This humility is a reflection of his deep loyalty, which is not about seeking recognition or reward but about serving Rama with complete selflessness.

Furthermore, Hanuman's loyalty is characterized by its absolute constancy. Throughout the Ramayana, there is never a moment of doubt, hesitation, or wavering in Hanuman's devotion to Rama. Even when faced with seemingly insurmountable obstacles or when confronted with the immense power of Ravana, Hanuman's faith in Rama remains unshaken. This constancy is a hallmark of true loyalty, which does not fluctuate with circumstances but remains steadfast regardless of external conditions.

The Nature of Selflessness: Hanuman's Complete Dedication to the Greater Good

Selflessness, the act of putting the needs and well-being of others before one's own, is another core aspect of Hanuman's character. While loyalty binds Hanuman to Rama, selflessness is what drives him to act in the best interests of others, often at great personal risk or sacrifice. Hanuman's selflessness is not just about his actions; it is a fundamental aspect of his identity, influencing every decision he makes and every challenge he undertakes.

One of the most striking examples of Hanuman's selflessness is his journey to the Himalayas to find the Sanjeevani herb to save Lakshmana's life. When Lakshmana is struck down by Ravana's son Indrajit, Rama is overcome with grief and despair. In this critical moment, Hanuman steps forward without a second thought, ready to undertake the arduous and dangerous mission of finding the magical herb that can save Lakshmana. The journey to the Himalayas is fraught with challenges, from the treacherous terrain to the immense pressure of time, yet Hanuman's focus remains solely on saving Lakshmana for Rama's sake.

What makes this episode particularly significant is Hanuman's decision to carry the entire mountain back to the battlefield when he is unable to identify the specific herb. This decision, made in the face of uncertainty, reflects Hanuman's selflessness and his commitment to doing whatever it takes to fulfill his mission. Hanuman's concern is not for his own safety or comfort but for the lives of others and the success of Rama's cause. His actions demonstrate the essence of selflessness—acting not for personal gain but for the benefit of others, even at great personal cost.

Another example of Hanuman's selflessness is seen in his encounter with the demoness Surasa during his flight to Lanka. Surasa, sent by the gods to test Hanuman, challenges him to enter her mouth as part of a divine mandate. Hanuman, understanding the nature of this test, does not resort to violence or seek to escape his fate. Instead, he uses his intelligence and humility to navigate the situation. By shrinking himself to a tiny size and entering and exiting Surasa's mouth swiftly, Hanuman fulfills the conditions of the test without causing harm to Surasa or himself. This episode highlights Hanuman's ability to prioritize the greater good over his own pride or power, choosing a path of selflessness and non-violence in service to his mission.

Moreover, Hanuman's selflessness is deeply connected to his understanding of dharma. He recognizes that his power and abilities are not for his own benefit but are meant to serve a higher purpose. This understanding is what drives Hanuman to undertake dangerous missions, face formidable enemies, and endure great hardships, all without seeking recognition or reward. For Hanuman, selflessness is not just a virtue; it is a way of life, a reflection of his deep connection to dharma and his role in the cosmic order.

Loyalty and Selflessness in Action: Hanuman's Role in the Battle of Lanka

The Battle of Lanka is one of the most intense and critical moments in the Ramayana, where the forces of good and evil clash in a final confrontation. Throughout this epic battle, Hanuman's loyalty and selflessness are on full display, as he plays a pivotal role in ensuring Rama's victory over Ravana.

Hanuman's loyalty to Rama is evident in his unwavering dedication on the battlefield. He fights with unparalleled courage and strength, not out of a desire for personal glory but to protect Rama and fulfill his duty. Hanuman's actions during the battle are characterized by a deep sense of responsibility and a willingness to go to any lengths to ensure the success of Rama's mission.

One of the most iconic moments in the battle is when Hanuman single-handedly takes on the mighty Kumbhakarna, Ravana's brother. Kumbhakarna is a formidable opponent, known for his immense strength and invincibility. Yet, Hanuman faces him without fear, motivated by his loyalty to Rama and his selfless desire to protect the vanara army and the cause of dharma.

Hanuman's victory over Kumbhakarna is not just a demonstration of his physical prowess but also a testament to his unwavering loyalty and selflessness. He fights not for his own survival but to uphold the principles of justice and righteousness.

Hanuman's selflessness is also evident in his care for the wounded and the fallen during the battle. Despite being a fierce warrior, Hanuman is equally compassionate, taking the time to tend to the injured and ensure that they receive the necessary care. His actions on the battlefield are not just about defeating the enemy but also about protecting and preserving life. This duality of being a warrior and a caretaker highlights the depth of Hanuman's selflessness, where he sees the value of every life and acts to preserve it whenever possible.

Furthermore, Hanuman's role as a messenger and diplomat during the battle underscores his loyalty and selflessness. When Rama needs to send messages to the vanara leaders or when there is a need to negotiate with Vibhishana or other allies, Hanuman steps forward to take on these tasks, understanding the importance of clear communication and strategic alliances. His willingness to serve in whatever capacity is needed, whether as a warrior, a healer, or a diplomat, reflects his deep commitment to the greater good and his selfless devotion to Rama's cause.

The Ultimate Test of Loyalty: Hanuman's Encounter with Bharata

One of the most profound tests of Hanuman's loyalty and selflessness occurs after the battle is won and Rama is on his way back to Ayodhya. As Rama's messenger, Hanuman is sent ahead to inform Bharata, Rama's brother, of their impending arrival. This encounter is significant because it reveals the depth of Hanuman's loyalty not just to Rama but to the entire family and the principles they stand for.

Bharata, who has been ruling Ayodhya in Rama's absence, is a paragon of dharma and devotion himself. Upon hearing the news of Rama's return, Bharata is overwhelmed with joy and gratitude. However, he also expresses a deep sorrow for the years lost and the suffering endured by Rama during his exile. Hanuman, understanding the complexity of Bharata's emotions, approaches him with great respect and empathy.

In this moment, Hanuman's loyalty to Rama is mirrored by his loyalty to Bharata, whom he sees as an extension of Rama's divine mission. Hanuman's words to Bharata are carefully chosen, reflecting his deep understanding of Bharata's character and the situation at hand. He reassures Bharata that Rama holds no resentment and that their reunion will bring about a new era of peace and prosperity for Ayodhya.

What makes this encounter particularly significant is Hanuman's selflessness in how he delivers the message. Despite his own fatigue and the trials he has endured, Hanuman's focus is entirely on alleviating Bharata's concerns and ensuring that the transition of power back to Rama is smooth and harmonious. Hanuman's ability to put aside his own experiences and focus on the well-being of others, even in moments of personal triumph, is a testament to his unparalleled selflessness.

Loyalty and Selflessness Beyond the Ramayana: Hanuman's Enduring Legacy

The qualities of loyalty and selflessness that define Hanuman's character are not confined to the events of the Ramayana; they continue to resonate in the cultural and spiritual traditions that have evolved around Hanuman over the centuries. Hanuman is not only a central figure in the Ramayana but also a beloved deity in his own right, worshipped for his virtues and his unwavering devotion to Rama.

In the countless temples dedicated to Hanuman across India and beyond, devotees seek to emulate his loyalty and selflessness in their own lives. Hanuman is often invoked for strength, courage, and protection, but equally important is his role as a model of perfect devotion and selfless service. His stories are recounted not just as tales of heroism but as moral and spiritual lessons that guide individuals in their own journeys.

Hanuman's legacy also extends to the world of art, literature, and performance. In traditional Indian dance and theater, the character of Hanuman is portrayed with a focus on his loyalty and selflessness, inspiring audiences with his virtues. In modern interpretations, Hanuman is often depicted as a symbol of resilience, humility, and unwavering commitment to truth and righteousness.

Moreover, Hanuman's qualities of loyalty and selflessness are seen as essential virtues in the practice of bhakti (devotional) traditions. In these traditions, Hanuman is revered not only as a hero of the Ramayana but as an ideal devotee, whose life is a testament to the power of selfless love and service. His story encourages devotees to cultivate a similar spirit of devotion and to live lives that are guided by principles of loyalty and selflessness.

The Relevance of Hanuman's Loyalty and Selflessness in Modern Times

In today's world, where individualism and self-interest often dominate, Hanuman's example of loyalty and selflessness offers a powerful counter-narrative. His story challenges the notion that success and fulfillment are achieved through personal ambition alone. Instead, Hanuman shows us that true greatness lies in our ability to serve others, to remain loyal to our principles and loved ones, and to act with selflessness in all that we do.

Hanuman's loyalty reminds us of the importance of commitment and fidelity in our relationships, whether they are personal, professional, or spiritual. In a time when loyalty is often tested by changing circumstances and shifting allegiances, Hanuman's unwavering devotion to Rama serves as a beacon of steadfastness and reliability. His example encourages us to remain true to our commitments, even when faced with challenges, and to honor the bonds that connect us to others.

Similarly, Hanuman's selflessness offers a powerful lesson in the value of service and altruism. In a world where success is often measured by what we can achieve for ourselves, Hanuman's life teaches us the profound fulfillment that comes from serving others and putting the needs of the greater good above our own. His story inspires us to act with generosity, compassion, and a sense of responsibility towards those around us.

Moreover, Hanuman's combination of loyalty and selflessness is a reminder that these qualities are not mutually exclusive but are deeply interconnected. True loyalty, as Hanuman demonstrates, is not about blind allegiance but about selflessly supporting and upholding the values and principles that define our relationships. Likewise, selflessness is not about self-neglect but about recognizing that our greatest strengths are realized when we act in the service of others and a higher purpose.

In conclusion, Hanuman's loyalty and selflessness are not just virtues to be admired from afar; they are qualities that we can strive to cultivate in our own lives. Through his unwavering devotion to Rama and his selfless dedication to the greater good, Hanuman embodies the highest ideals of loyalty and selflessness. His legacy continues to inspire and guide us, offering timeless lessons on how to live lives that are meaningful, purposeful, and deeply connected to the well-being of others. In a world that often emphasizes personal success and individualism, Hanuman's example reminds us that true greatness is found in our capacity to serve, to remain loyal to our principles and loved ones, and to act with selflessness in all that we do.

CHAPTER X

Hanuman as a Yogi and Sage

Spiritual Strength: The Path of Self-Mastery and Inner Peace

The figure of Hanuman in the Ramayana is often celebrated for his immense physical strength, boundless devotion, and unwavering loyalty to Lord Rama. However, beneath this exterior lies a profound spiritual depth that characterizes Hanuman not only as a warrior and devotee but also as a yogi and sage of the highest order. Hanuman embodies the ideals of a perfected being, who, through discipline, devotion, and self-realization, attains a state of unity with the divine. This chapter explores the lesser-known aspects of Hanuman's character as a yogi and sage, delving into his spiritual practices, his embodiment of yogic principles, and the wisdom he imparts as a realized being.

The Yogi's Discipline: Hanuman's Mastery Over Mind and Body

The essence of yoga lies in the mastery of the mind and body, leading to the union of the individual self with the divine consciousness. Hanuman's life is a testament to this mastery. While his feats of strength and agility are well-known, they are underpinned by an extraordinary control over his physical and mental faculties, which is the hallmark of a true yogi.

Hanuman's physical prowess, as described in the Ramayana, is not merely a result of his divine heritage as the son of Vayu, the wind god, but also of his disciplined practice of yoga. The control he exhibits over his body is evident in his ability to expand and contract his size at will, a skill known as *Mahima* and *Anima*, which are among the *ashta siddhis* (eight supernatural powers) mentioned in yogic texts. This control over his physical form symbolizes Hanuman's mastery over the material world, which he can transcend at will.

Moreover, Hanuman's control over his mind is perhaps even more remarkable. As a yogi, he embodies the principle of *vairagya* (detachment), which allows him to remain unperturbed by the dualities of pleasure and pain, success and failure, or praise and blame. This detachment is not a lack of emotion or concern but a profound equanimity that comes from the realization that all experiences, whether positive or negative, are transient and ultimately illusory.

One of the clearest examples of Hanuman's mental discipline is seen in his encounter with Surasa, the demoness who tries to obstruct his journey to Lanka. Hanuman faces this challenge with remarkable calm and presence of mind. Instead of engaging in a direct confrontation, he uses his yogic powers to shrink his size, entering and exiting her mouth in a matter of seconds. This act of self-shrinking is not just a display of physical ability but a demonstration of Hanuman's control over his ego, reducing it to nothingness in the face of adversity. This incident highlights Hanuman's ability to remain composed and focused in the midst of challenges, a quality that is essential for any yogi.

Hanuman's mastery over his mind is also reflected in his unwavering focus on his duties and his devotion to Rama. Despite the numerous distractions and temptations that come his way, Hanuman remains steadfast in his purpose. This singular focus, known as *ekagrata* in yogic terms, is crucial for the attainment of higher states of consciousness. Hanuman's ability to maintain this focus is a reflection of his deep meditative practice and his commitment to the path of yoga.

The Sage's Wisdom: Hanuman's Insights into Dharma and the Self

As a sage, Hanuman's wisdom is rooted in his profound understanding of dharma (righteousness) and the nature of the self. Hanuman is not only a warrior who fights for justice but also a teacher and guide who imparts spiritual wisdom to those around him. His insights are not just theoretical knowledge but are born out of direct experience and realization.

Hanuman's understanding of dharma is comprehensive and nuanced. He recognizes that dharma is not a rigid code of conduct but a dynamic principle that must be applied with discernment and compassion. This is evident in his interactions with various characters in the Ramayana, where Hanuman often acts as a mediator, offering counsel that is both practical and aligned with higher principles.

One of the most profound examples of Hanuman's wisdom is seen in his conversation with Vibhishana, Ravana's brother. When Vibhishana seeks refuge with Rama, the vanaras are initially suspicious of his intentions. It is Hanuman who steps forward to engage with Vibhishana, carefully assessing his sincerity and intentions. Hanuman's ability to see beyond surface appearances and discern the true nature of a person reflects his deep understanding of dharma. He recognizes that Vibhishana's defection from Ravana's side is not an act of betrayal but a courageous decision to uphold righteousness. Hanuman's support for Vibhishana's asylum is a testament to his ability to apply dharma with wisdom and compassion, rather than rigidly adhering to conventional norms.

Hanuman's wisdom also extends to his understanding of the self and the nature of reality. As a realized being, Hanuman is fully aware of his divine nature and his oneness with the universal consciousness. This realization is what allows him to perform seemingly impossible feats with ease and grace, as he knows that he is not limited by his physical form but is an expression of the infinite divine.

One of the most striking illustrations of Hanuman's self-realization is his response to Sita's question about his identity.

When Sita asks Hanuman who he is, Hanuman responds by describing himself in three different ways, depending on his state of consciousness. He says, "When I do not know who I am, I serve you, O Rama. When I do know who I am, you are I, and I am you. And when I am fully established in the realization of my true self, I am neither you nor I, but the one undivided consciousness." This profound statement encapsulates Hanuman's understanding of the different levels of consciousness and his realization of the non-dual nature of reality.

Hanuman's wisdom is not just limited to spiritual insights but also encompasses practical knowledge and skills. His ability to strategize, negotiate, and inspire others is a reflection of his comprehensive understanding of the world and its workings. Whether it is planning the construction of the bridge to Lanka, advising Rama on military tactics, or encouraging the vanaras in battle, Hanuman's actions are guided by a deep wisdom that integrates both spiritual and worldly knowledge.

Hanuman and the Path of Bhakti Yoga

While Hanuman is often associated with physical prowess and intellectual wisdom, his greatest legacy is perhaps his role as the ultimate bhakta (devotee). Hanuman's life is a living embodiment of bhakti yoga, the path of devotion, which seeks union with the divine through love and surrender. For Hanuman, every action, thought, and breath is an offering to Lord Rama, whom he worships with absolute devotion and selflessness.

Hanuman's devotion to Rama is not just an emotional attachment but a profound spiritual practice that transforms his entire being. In bhakti yoga, the devotee seeks to dissolve the ego and merge with the divine, and Hanuman achieves this through his unwavering love and service to Rama. His devotion is characterized by three key aspects: surrender, service, and selflessness.

The first aspect of Hanuman's bhakti is complete surrender (*sharanagati*). Hanuman surrenders not only his actions but also his will and identity to Rama. This surrender is not an act of weakness or passivity but a conscious choice to align his individual will with the divine will. Hanuman's surrender is evident in his famous declaration to Rama: "I am your servant, and I exist only to serve you. My life, my strength, my everything belongs to you." This statement encapsulates the essence of bhakti, where the devotee relinquishes all sense of personal ownership and dedicates everything to the divine.

The second aspect of Hanuman's bhakti is service (*seva*). Hanuman's devotion to Rama is expressed through his tireless service, which he performs with joy and enthusiasm, regardless of the difficulty or danger involved. Whether it is crossing the ocean to find Sita, fighting in the battle of Lanka, or carrying the Sanjeevani herb to save Lakshmana, Hanuman's actions are driven by his desire to serve Rama and fulfill his divine mission. For Hanuman, service is not a duty but a privilege, an opportunity to express his love and devotion to Rama.

The third aspect of Hanuman's bhakti is selflessness (*nishkama karma*). Hanuman's actions are devoid of any desire for personal gain or recognition. He acts purely out of love for Rama, without any expectation of reward or acknowledgment. This selflessness is what makes Hanuman's devotion so pure and powerful. In bhakti yoga, selfless service is considered the highest form of worship, and Hanuman exemplifies this principle in every aspect of his life.

Hanuman's role as a bhakta is not limited to his relationship with Rama but extends to his interactions with others as well. His compassion, humility, and willingness to help others, regardless of their status or background, reflect his deep commitment to the principles of bhakti. Hanuman's devotion is not exclusive but inclusive, embracing all beings as manifestations of the divine.

In many ways, Hanuman's devotion to Rama serves as a model for all devotees, regardless of their spiritual path. His example shows that true bhakti is not about ritualistic worship or emotional fervor but about a deep, abiding love for the divine that permeates every aspect of one's life. Hanuman's life teaches us that devotion is not just about what we do in the temple or in prayer but about how we live our lives, how we treat others, and how we align our will with the divine will.

Hanuman's Role in Advaita Vedanta: The Non-Dual Sage

While Hanuman is most commonly associated with the path of bhakti, his life and teachings also resonate with the principles of Advaita Vedanta, the philosophy of non-dualism. Advaita Vedanta teaches that the individual self (*jivatman*) is not separate from the supreme self (*Paramatman*), and that the ultimate goal of life is to realize this oneness with the divine.

Hanuman's realization of non-duality is evident in his understanding of his relationship with Rama. While he serves Rama as his devoted servant, he is also aware that Rama and he are not separate but are one in essence. This understanding is what allows Hanuman to perform his superhuman feats, as he knows that he is not limited by his individual identity but is an expression of the infinite divine.

Hanuman's realization of non-duality is also reflected in his actions, which are characterized by a sense of unity and harmony with the world around him. He does not see himself as separate from others but recognizes the divine presence in all beings. This awareness of the oneness of all life is what enables Hanuman to act with compassion, humility, and wisdom, as he sees all beings as part of the same divine consciousness.

In the context of Advaita Vedanta, Hanuman's life can be seen as an example of *jivanmukti* – the state of liberation while still living in the body. A *jivanmukta* is one who has realized the non-dual nature of reality and lives in a state of constant awareness of the divine. Hanuman's life embodies this state of *jivanmukti*, as he moves through the world with complete freedom and detachment, acting selflessly and without any sense of personal doership.

Hanuman's role as a non-dual sage is further emphasized in the *Hanuman Chalisa*, a devotional hymn that praises Hanuman's virtues and achievements. In the *Chalisa*, Hanuman is described as the knower of all knowledge, the master of all sciences, and the destroyer of all obstacles. These descriptions highlight Hanuman's realization of the ultimate truth and his ability to transcend the limitations of the material world.

Moreover, Hanuman's ability to switch effortlessly between his roles as a servant, a warrior, a sage, and a divine being reflects his non-dual awareness. He does not identify with any particular role or form but moves fluidly between them, guided by the needs of the moment and the will of the divine. This flexibility and adaptability are hallmarks of a realized being who is not bound by any fixed identity or concept.

The Symbolism of Hanuman as a Yogi and Sage

In addition to his roles as a yogi and sage, Hanuman is also a powerful symbol of spiritual ideals and aspirations. His form and attributes are rich with symbolic meaning, offering insights into the deeper dimensions of his character and the qualities he represents.

Hanuman's monkey form, for example, symbolizes the restless and playful nature of the mind, which can be harnessed and transformed through the practice of yoga. The monkey is often seen as a creature of curiosity, mischief, and boundless energy, and in many ways, it represents the untamed mind that jumps from one thought to another, driven by desires and impulses. Hanuman's mastery over his monkey nature symbolizes the yogi's ability to control and direct the mind towards higher spiritual goals.

Hanuman's tail, which is often depicted as long and powerful, symbolizes the kundalini energy, which lies dormant at the base of the spine and can be awakened through yogic practices. When this energy rises, it leads to higher states of consciousness and spiritual awakening. Hanuman's burning of Lanka with his tail can be seen as a metaphor for the awakening of kundalini and the destruction of ignorance and ego that comes with it.

Hanuman's heart, which is often depicted as containing the images of Rama and Sita, symbolizes his pure and unwavering devotion. The image of Rama and Sita in Hanuman's heart represents the union of the individual self with the divine, which is the ultimate goal of bhakti yoga. Hanuman's open heart also symbolizes his transparency and sincerity, as he has nothing to hide and no personal agenda, but lives only to serve and love the divine.

Hanuman's mace, which he carries as a weapon, symbolizes the power of knowledge and discrimination (*viveka*). The mace is a symbol of strength, but in Hanuman's hands, it is also a tool for destroying ignorance and falsehood. Hanuman uses his mace not to harm others but to protect dharma and uphold righteousness. This symbolizes the yogi's use of knowledge not for self-aggrandizement but for the service of the greater good.

Finally, Hanuman's leap to Lanka, in which he crosses the ocean in a single bound, symbolizes the yogi's ability to transcend the limitations of the material world and reach the shores of spiritual realization. The ocean represents the vast and seemingly insurmountable challenges of life, while Hanuman's leap symbolizes the power of faith, devotion, and self-realization to overcome these challenges and attain the ultimate goal of union with the divine.

The Legacy of Hanuman as a Yogi and Sage

Hanuman's legacy as a yogi and sage continues to inspire spiritual seekers across generations and cultures. His life and teachings offer a timeless example of how to live a life of devotion, wisdom, and self-realization, while also engaging fully with the world and fulfilling one's duties.

In the practice of yoga, Hanuman is revered as an ideal practitioner who embodies the highest principles of yogic discipline, control, and devotion. His life teaches us that yoga is not just a physical practice but a way of life that involves the cultivation of virtues such as self-control, focus, compassion, and wisdom. Hanuman's mastery over his body and mind, his deep understanding of dharma, and his unwavering devotion to the divine make him a role model for anyone on the spiritual path.

In the broader context of Indian spirituality, Hanuman is also seen as a symbol of the ideal devotee and the perfect servant of God. His life exemplifies the principles of bhakti yoga, showing us that true devotion involves not just ritualistic worship but a complete surrender of the self to the divine will. Hanuman's selfless service, his humility, and his unwavering loyalty to Rama serve as powerful reminders of the transformative power of love and devotion.

Moreover, Hanuman's realization of non-duality and his embodiment of Advaita Vedanta principles make him a revered figure in the tradition of non-dualism. His life demonstrates that the highest spiritual realization involves seeing the divine in all beings and recognizing the oneness of all life. Hanuman's actions, guided by wisdom and compassion, reflect the principles of non-duality in action, showing us that true spirituality involves not just inner realization but also outer service to the world.

Hanuman's legacy also extends beyond the realm of Indian spirituality, as his qualities of strength, devotion, and wisdom have universal appeal. In the modern world, where people are often faced with challenges, distractions, and conflicts, Hanuman's example offers valuable lessons on how to live a life of purpose, integrity, and spiritual depth. His life teaches us that true strength comes from self-control and discipline, true wisdom comes from understanding and compassion, and true devotion comes from love and surrender to the divine.

In conclusion, Hanuman's role as a yogi and sage is a profound aspect of his character that offers rich insights into the deeper dimensions of his life and teachings. Through his mastery over mind and body, his wisdom and understanding of dharma, his devotion to Rama, and his realization of non-duality, Hanuman embodies the ideals of a perfected being who has attained union with the divine. His life continues to inspire and guide spiritual seekers, offering timeless lessons on how to live a life of devotion, wisdom, and self-realization in the midst of the challenges and responsibilities of the world. Hanuman's legacy as a yogi and sage is a testament to the transformative power of yoga and devotion, and his example remains a beacon of light for all those on the spiritual path.

CHAPTER XI

Hanuman in the Modern World

Living Hanuman's Values Today: How His Teachings Inspire Modern Society

In the ancient texts of the Ramayana and Mahabharata, Hanuman emerges as a powerful figure of devotion, strength, and wisdom, embodying the highest ideals of loyalty, service, and spiritual realization. But beyond his role in these epic narratives, Hanuman's presence continues to resonate in the modern world, where his qualities offer deep insights and inspiration for contemporary life. This chapter explores Hanuman's relevance in today's context, examining how his virtues can be applied to the challenges and opportunities of the modern world. It delves into how Hanuman's attributes—such as his unwavering devotion, boundless strength, profound wisdom, humility, and adaptability—serve as a guide for navigating the complexities of modern existence.

The Universal Appeal of Hanuman's Devotion

One of Hanuman's most enduring qualities is his unwavering devotion to Lord Rama. In an era where materialism and self-centeredness often dominate, Hanuman's example of selfless devotion stands out as a reminder of the power of love and service to something greater than oneself. In the modern world, where the pursuit of individual success can sometimes lead to isolation and disconnection, Hanuman's devotion encourages us to look beyond our personal desires and align our lives with a higher purpose.

In the context of contemporary spirituality, Hanuman's devotion can be seen as an invitation to cultivate a deeper connection with the divine, however one may conceive it. For some, this may involve a commitment to religious or spiritual practices, while for others, it might mean dedicating themselves to causes that serve the greater good, such as social justice, environmental sustainability, or humanitarian efforts. Hanuman's life teaches that true fulfillment comes not from selfish pursuits, but from the joy of serving others and contributing to the well-being of the world.

Moreover, Hanuman's devotion is characterized by a profound sense of surrender. In a time when control and power are often prized, Hanuman reminds us of the strength that lies in letting go of our need to dominate or manipulate outcomes. His surrender to Lord Rama was not a sign of weakness, but rather a testament to his trust in the divine will. In the modern world, this surrender can be interpreted as an acceptance of life's uncertainties and challenges, trusting that there is a greater plan at work, even when things do not go as we had hoped.

Hanuman's devotion also exemplifies the concept of *bhakti yoga*, the path of love and devotion, which is particularly relevant in today's world where people are searching for meaning and connection amidst the distractions of daily life. Through his example, Hanuman shows that devotion is not just about worship or ritual, but about living a life that reflects one's highest values and commitments. In this way, Hanuman serves as a role model for those who seek to live with integrity, compassion, and purpose in a world that often values superficial success over deeper spiritual fulfillment.

Strength and Resilience in the Face of Modern Challenges

In a world that is increasingly complex and demanding, Hanuman's strength and resilience offer powerful lessons for overcoming obstacles and persevering in the face of adversity. Hanuman's physical strength, which enabled him to perform extraordinary feats such as leaping across the ocean to Lanka or carrying the mountain of medicinal herbs to save Lakshmana, is a metaphor for the inner strength that each of us can cultivate to face the challenges of life.

Hanuman's strength is not merely physical; it is also mental and emotional. He exemplifies the power of determination, courage, and resilience, qualities that are essential for navigating the difficulties of modern life. In a world where stress, anxiety, and burnout are common, Hanuman's example teaches us the importance of building inner strength through practices such as meditation, mindfulness, and self-discipline. By cultivating these qualities, we can develop the resilience needed to face life's challenges with grace and equanimity.

Moreover, Hanuman's strength is deeply rooted in his sense of purpose. He is able to perform his extraordinary feats because he is driven by a deep commitment to his mission—serving Lord Rama and fulfilling his divine duty. In the modern world, where many people struggle with a sense of meaninglessness or lack of direction, Hanuman's example shows the importance of having a clear sense of purpose. Whether it is in our careers, relationships, or personal growth, having a strong sense of purpose can provide the motivation and strength needed to overcome obstacles and achieve our goals.

Hanuman's strength also teaches us about the power of faith. His unwavering belief in Rama's mission gives him the courage to face even the most daunting challenges without hesitation. In the modern world, where doubt and skepticism often prevail, Hanuman's faith serves as a reminder of the importance of believing in something greater than ourselves. This faith can be in a higher power, in the goodness of humanity, or in our own potential to overcome difficulties. By cultivating faith, we can find the inner strength to persevere, even when the odds seem insurmountable.

Wisdom and Discernment in a Complex World

Hanuman is not only a figure of strength and devotion but also of profound wisdom and discernment. In the Ramayana, his actions are always guided by deep understanding and careful judgment, whether it is in his interactions with allies and enemies, his strategic decisions in battle, or his counsel to others. In the modern world, where information overload and rapid change can lead to confusion and poor decision-making, Hanuman's wisdom offers valuable lessons in how to navigate complexity with clarity and insight.

One of the key aspects of Hanuman's wisdom is his ability to see the bigger picture. He is not swayed by emotions or immediate circumstances, but always considers the long-term consequences of his actions. This quality is particularly important in today's world, where short-term thinking often leads to decisions that may be expedient in the moment but detrimental in the long run. Hanuman's example encourages us to cultivate foresight and to make decisions that are not only beneficial for ourselves but also for others and for the future.

Hanuman's wisdom is also characterized by his ability to discern the truth. In the Ramayana, he often plays the role of a mediator, helping to resolve conflicts and guide others towards the right course of action. His ability to see through deception and recognize the underlying reality of situations is a reflection of his deep understanding of dharma, the cosmic law of righteousness. In the modern world, where misinformation and manipulation are rampant, Hanuman's discernment is a reminder of the importance of seeking truth and acting with integrity.

Furthermore, Hanuman's wisdom is deeply connected to his humility. Despite his extraordinary abilities, Hanuman never allows pride or ego to cloud his judgment. He is always willing to learn from others and to act in the best interests of those he serves, rather than seeking recognition for himself. This humility is a key aspect of wisdom, as it allows us to remain open to new perspectives and to make decisions based on what is truly right, rather than what will enhance our own status or power. In a world where ego and self-interest often drive decision-making, Hanuman's humility offers a powerful counterexample of how true wisdom is grounded in selflessness and service to others.

Hanuman as a Symbol of Adaptability and Change

One of the most remarkable aspects of Hanuman's character is his adaptability. Throughout the Ramayana, Hanuman demonstrates an ability to adjust to different situations and challenges with ease, whether it is shrinking to the size of a fly to enter Lanka unnoticed or expanding to a giant size to challenge the demons. This adaptability is not just a physical ability but also a reflection of Hanuman's mental and emotional flexibility, which allows him to respond to changing circumstances with creativity and resourcefulness.

In the modern world, where change is constant and often unpredictable, Hanuman's adaptability is a valuable quality to emulate. Whether it is in our personal lives, careers, or social environments, the ability to adapt to new situations is essential for success and well-being. Hanuman's example teaches us that adaptability is not about abandoning our principles or goals but about finding new ways to achieve them in the face of changing circumstances.

Hanuman's adaptability is also closely linked to his resilience. He is able to bounce back from setbacks and challenges because he does not cling to a fixed idea of how things should be. Instead, he remains open to new possibilities and is willing to change his approach when necessary. In the modern world, where rigidity and resistance to change can lead to frustration and failure, Hanuman's flexibility offers a powerful lesson in how to navigate life's uncertainties with grace and resilience.

Moreover, Hanuman's adaptability is grounded in his deep sense of identity and purpose. He is able to adjust to different situations without losing sight of who he is or what he stands for. This balance between flexibility and stability is a key aspect of effective adaptability. In the modern world, where identity and values are often challenged by external pressures, Hanuman's example shows the importance of staying true to oneself while being open to change.

Hanuman's Humility and Leadership in a Competitive World

Despite his immense power and accomplishments, Hanuman is renowned for his humility. He never seeks personal glory or recognition, always attributing his successes to the grace of Lord Rama. This humility is a core aspect of Hanuman's greatness, setting him apart as a leader who serves rather than dominates. In the modern world, where leadership is often equated with assertiveness and control, Hanuman's humility offers a different model of leadership based on service, compassion, and selflessness.

Hanuman's humility is evident in the way he interacts with others. He treats everyone with respect, regardless of their status or abilities, and is always willing to listen and learn. This approach to leadership is particularly relevant in today's world, where collaborative and inclusive leadership styles are increasingly recognized as more effective than authoritarian ones. Hanuman's example shows that true leadership is not about exerting power over others but about empowering them to achieve their best.

Furthermore, Hanuman's humility allows him to remain focused on his mission without being distracted by ego or pride. In a competitive world where success is often measured by personal achievements and accolades, Hanuman's detachment from self-interest serves as a reminder of the importance of staying committed to one's higher purpose. His example encourages us to lead with integrity, prioritizing the greater good over personal gain, and to recognize that true success lies in the impact we have on others and the world around us.

Hanuman's humility also contributes to his ability to inspire and uplift others. His selflessness and dedication to Rama make him a beloved figure not only in the Ramayana but also in the hearts of those who revere him. In the modern world, where leaders are often judged by their charisma and influence, Hanuman's example shows that the most enduring form of leadership comes from the ability to inspire others through one's character and actions, rather than through force or persuasion.

Hanuman's Role in Cultural and Spiritual Practices

Hanuman's influence extends far beyond the pages of the Ramayana; he is a central figure in Hindu worship and cultural practices across the world. Temples dedicated to Hanuman are found throughout India and in many other countries, where devotees offer prayers and perform rituals to seek his blessings. Hanuman's presence in the modern world is a testament to the enduring power of his character and the deep resonance of his qualities with the spiritual aspirations of millions.

In contemporary Hinduism, Hanuman is revered as a protector and a source of strength. Devotees often pray to Hanuman for courage, health, and protection from harm, particularly in times of crisis. The *Hanuman Chalisa*, a devotional hymn dedicated to Hanuman, is recited daily by millions of people as a way of invoking his blessings and guidance. This practice reflects the belief that Hanuman's presence is not limited to the past but is an active force in the lives of those who seek his help.

Moreover, Hanuman's role in spiritual practices is not confined to Hinduism. His qualities of devotion, strength, and wisdom have universal appeal, making him a figure of inspiration in various spiritual traditions. In the modern world, where people are increasingly seeking spirituality beyond the boundaries of organized religion, Hanuman's example offers a model of spiritual practice that is accessible to all. His emphasis on devotion, service, and humility provides a pathway for spiritual growth that transcends religious boundaries, offering a source of inspiration for people of all faiths.

In addition to his role in worship and spiritual practice, Hanuman is also a prominent figure in cultural expressions such as art, literature, and performance. His stories are told and retold in various forms, from classical dance and theater to modern films and television shows. These cultural expressions keep Hanuman's legacy alive and relevant, allowing new generations to connect with his story and values in ways that resonate with their own experiences.

Hanuman as a Symbol of Unity and Social Justice

In a world that is increasingly divided along lines of race, religion, and nationality, Hanuman's life and teachings offer a powerful symbol of unity and social justice. Throughout the Ramayana, Hanuman is shown interacting with a diverse range of characters, from kings and warriors to sages and common folk, always treating them with respect and compassion. His actions reflect a deep understanding of the interconnectedness of all beings and the importance of working together for the common good.

Hanuman's role as a unifier is particularly relevant in the modern world, where social divisions and conflicts often lead to violence and injustice. His example teaches us that true strength lies not in dominating others but in bringing people together and working for the well-being of all. In this way, Hanuman can be seen as a symbol of social justice, advocating for a society where all people are treated with dignity and respect, regardless of their background or status.

Moreover, Hanuman's humility and service-oriented leadership offer a model for addressing social issues in a way that is inclusive and compassionate. In the modern world, where power dynamics often lead to exploitation and inequality, Hanuman's example shows that true leadership is about lifting others up rather than asserting control. His life teaches us that social justice is not just about fighting against injustice, but also about creating a society where everyone has the opportunity to thrive and fulfill their potential.

Hanuman's legacy as a symbol of unity and social justice is further emphasized by his role in the Indian independence movement, where he was invoked as a symbol of resistance against colonial rule. Leaders like Mahatma Gandhi and Subhas Chandra Bose drew inspiration from Hanuman's courage and strength, seeing in him a figure who embodied the ideals of freedom and justice. In this way, Hanuman's influence extends beyond the spiritual realm into the political and social arenas, where his example continues to inspire those who fight for justice and equality.

The Enduring Legacy of Hanuman in the Modern World

Hanuman's presence in the modern world is a testament to the timeless relevance of his qualities and teachings. Whether it is through his devotion, strength, wisdom, humility, adaptability, or commitment to social justice, Hanuman offers valuable lessons for navigating the challenges and opportunities of contemporary life. His example teaches us that true success and fulfillment come not from selfish pursuits but from living a life of purpose, integrity, and service to others.

In a world that is often characterized by materialism, competition, and division, Hanuman's legacy serves as a powerful reminder of the importance of spiritual values such as love, compassion, and humility. His life shows us that these values are not just abstract ideals but practical qualities that can guide our actions and decisions in everyday life. By embodying these qualities, we can find the strength and wisdom to face the challenges of the modern world and to live lives that are meaningful, fulfilling, and aligned with our highest aspirations.

Furthermore, Hanuman's influence in the modern world is a reflection of the enduring power of myth and symbolism in human life. His stories continue to inspire and uplift people across cultures and generations, offering a source of hope and guidance in times of difficulty. Whether we encounter Hanuman in a temple, in a work of art, or in the stories passed down through generations, his presence reminds us of the eternal truths that underlie our existence and the potential we all have to rise above our limitations and achieve greatness.

In conclusion, Hanuman's relevance in the modern world is a reflection of the timeless qualities he embodies and the universal values he represents. His life offers a model of how to live with devotion, strength, wisdom, and humility in a world that is often filled with challenges and distractions. By following Hanuman's example, we can find the inspiration and guidance needed to navigate the complexities of modern life and to live in a way that is true to our highest ideals. Hanuman's legacy continues to shine as a beacon of hope and wisdom, offering timeless lessons for all who seek to live with purpose, integrity, and spiritual depth in the modern world.

CHAPTER XII

Hanuman's Eternal Life and Immortality

Beyond Time: The Immortal Values of Selflessness, Courage, and Faith

The concept of immortality is often associated with unattainable aspirations for humans, but in the Hindu epic tradition, certain beings have transcended death to become eternal. Lord Hanuman, the mighty devotee of Lord Rama, stands as one of these immortals, whose life and deeds have far-reaching implications not only in mythology but also in the realm of human existence. Hanuman's immortality goes beyond mere physical survival; it is a testament to his timeless virtues, such as loyalty, humility, courage, and selflessness. His eternal presence represents the power of devotion and dharma (righteousness) to transcend time, space, and death itself.

This chapter delves deeply into the nature of Hanuman's immortality and its broader implications for human life, focusing on the motivational and spiritual lessons that can be drawn from his eternal existence. Through a thorough exploration of Hanuman's journey to immortality and the symbolic power of his eternal life, this chapter offers insights into how modern individuals can incorporate his values into their lives, achieving their own form of immortality by living in alignment with higher principles.

The Boon of Immortality: Hanuman's Divine Blessing

Hanuman's immortality is a central theme in Hindu mythology, where he is considered one of the **Chiranjeevis**—the seven immortal beings in Hindu lore who are destined to live until the end of the current cosmic age. According to the Ramayana and other sacred texts, after the events of the great war between Rama and Ravana, Hanuman was granted the boon of immortality as a reward for his unwavering devotion, loyalty, and service to Lord Rama. This blessing was bestowed by Lord Rama himself, who declared that as long as people worship him, Hanuman's name would also be chanted and remembered. Thus, Hanuman's immortality is directly linked to his devotion and his role as a protector of dharma.

However, Hanuman's immortality is not to be understood merely in the literal sense of living forever. It is a symbol of his eternal relevance, his capacity to transcend the limitations of time, and his unbreakable connection to the divine. Hanuman's immortality is intertwined with his virtues—he is not immortal because of his physical strength or heroic deeds alone, but because of his humility, his willingness to serve, and his deep, abiding faith. This is a powerful lesson for human beings: it is not physical prowess or material success that grants immortality, but the cultivation of virtues that align with higher ideals.

For modern individuals, the message here is clear: the path to immortality lies not in the quest for endless life but in the pursuit of a life that is filled with meaning, purpose, and service to others. Just as Hanuman's name is immortalized through his devotion to Lord Rama, humans can achieve a form of immortality by living in ways that have a lasting positive impact on the world, ensuring that their legacy endures long after their physical presence has passed.

The Symbolism of Immortality: A Metaphor for Human Potential

Hanuman's immortality also serves as a powerful metaphor for human potential. In his stories, Hanuman is often depicted as forgetting his own strength and abilities until reminded by others. This forgetfulness is symbolic of the human condition, where individuals often underestimate their own potential and fail to realize their inner power. Hanuman's journey of rediscovering his strength and his eventual immortality can be seen as a reflection of the human capacity to overcome limitations, both physical and mental, by tapping into their latent potential.

In this sense, Hanuman's immortality represents the limitless possibilities that lie within each individual. His life is a reminder that true strength is not just physical, but comes from an unwavering commitment to righteousness and devotion. By aligning oneself with higher ideals, as Hanuman did with Lord Rama, individuals can transcend their perceived limitations and achieve greatness.

This is particularly motivating for humans because it suggests that immortality—symbolized by lasting significance or spiritual transcendence—is not reserved for divine beings alone. Instead, anyone can attain a form of immortality by realizing their inner potential, living a life of integrity, and dedicating themselves to a cause greater than their own self-interest. By doing so, their actions, values, and legacy will endure in the hearts and minds of future generations.

Hanuman's Eternal Life: A Model for Living in the Present

While Hanuman's immortality is often understood in terms of his eternal existence, it also offers a profound lesson about living fully in the present moment. Hanuman's life is characterized by complete mindfulness and focus on the task at hand. Whether it was leaping across the ocean to Lanka or carrying the mountain of herbs to save Lakshmana, Hanuman demonstrated an extraordinary ability to immerse himself fully in the moment, without being distracted by fear, doubt, or the potential consequences of failure. His immortality, then, is not just about eternal life after death but about being fully present and alive in every moment.

For human beings, this is an invaluable lesson. In today's fast-paced world, where distractions are everywhere and anxiety about the future often dominates our thoughts, Hanuman's ability to live fully in the present serves as a model for mindful living. Immortality, in this sense, is about experiencing life fully, without being bound by the fear of what is to come or the regrets of the past. By embracing the present moment and dedicating oneself wholeheartedly to whatever task is at hand, individuals can achieve a sense of timelessness in their daily lives.

Moreover, Hanuman's single-minded devotion to Lord Rama serves as a reminder that when we commit ourselves to a higher purpose, we can transcend the limitations of time and space. In Hanuman's case, his devotion made him an eternal servant of Lord Rama, ensuring his relevance across the ages. Similarly, when humans commit themselves to meaningful causes, whether it be serving others, fighting for justice, or contributing to the betterment of society, their actions create a lasting legacy that outlives their physical bodies.

Overcoming the Fear of Death: Hanuman's Fearlessness as a Model

Another important aspect of Hanuman's immortality is his complete lack of fear, particularly the fear of death. Throughout the Ramayana, Hanuman demonstrates extraordinary courage in the face of seemingly insurmountable obstacles. Whether he is confronting the mighty demon Ravana or entering the enemy territory of Lanka, Hanuman approaches each challenge with a fearless spirit. This fearlessness is not rooted in arrogance or recklessness but in his deep faith in Lord Rama and his unwavering belief in the righteousness of his mission.

For humans, fear of death is one of the most primal and deeply ingrained fears. Hanuman's example offers a way to transcend this fear by focusing on higher principles. Hanuman is fearless because he knows that his actions are aligned with dharma, and as long as he is serving a righteous cause, death holds no power over him. His immortality, therefore, is not just a divine boon but a result of his fearlessness and his deep understanding of life and death.

This is a profound source of motivation for human beings. It suggests that when we align our lives with higher principles—whether they be devotion, justice, love, or service—we too can transcend the fear of death. By focusing on the greater purpose of our existence, we can find the strength to face life's challenges with courage and determination, knowing that even in death, our legacy will endure.

The Power of Bhakti: Hanuman's Devotion as the Key to Immortality

At the heart of Hanuman's immortality is his unparalleled devotion, or *bhakti*, to Lord Rama. Bhakti, in the Hindu tradition, is a path of complete surrender and love for the divine, and Hanuman is often cited as the ultimate exemplar of this form of devotion. His every thought, word, and action is dedicated to Lord Rama, and it is this unwavering devotion that grants him the boon of eternal life.

For human beings, Hanuman's devotion offers a powerful lesson about the transformative power of love and service. By dedicating oneself to a cause greater than the self, individuals can transcend their limitations and achieve a sense of immortality. This could be devotion to a spiritual path, but it could also be a commitment to serving others, contributing to the welfare of society, or working toward a noble goal. The key is to act selflessly, as Hanuman did, without attachment to personal gain or recognition.

In this way, Hanuman's immortality is not just a divine blessing but a reflection of the universal truth that selfless love and devotion can transcend time. His life reminds us that true immortality is not found in the pursuit of personal glory but in dedicating ourselves to something greater, something eternal.

Hanuman as a Symbol of Hope and Resilience

Hanuman's immortality also symbolizes hope and resilience, particularly in the face of adversity. Throughout the Ramayana,

Hanuman encounters numerous challenges, from crossing the ocean to infiltrating Ravana's stronghold in Lanka. Each of these challenges represents a test of his strength, courage, and devotion. Yet, no matter how daunting the obstacles before him, Hanuman never gives up. His immortal nature is not just about living forever, but about his ability to rise again and again in the face of difficulties.

For modern readers, this is perhaps one of the most inspiring aspects of Hanuman's immortality. His story teaches us that resilience is a key to overcoming life's challenges. Even when the odds seem impossible, Hanuman's unwavering determination and faith allow him to prevail. This resilience, combined with his eternal life, sends a powerful message that difficulties are temporary, but the spirit that confronts them can be timeless.

Human beings can draw immense motivation from this. In the face of personal, professional, or spiritual struggles, Hanuman's example reminds us to stay resilient and to keep moving forward, knowing that our efforts, if aligned with righteousness and truth, will have lasting significance. Just as Hanuman overcame every obstacle in his path, we too can rise above our challenges and, in doing so, create a lasting impact on the world around us.

Conclusion: Immortality through Virtue

In conclusion, Hanuman's immortality is not just a divine gift but a reflection of the highest virtues he embodies—devotion, selflessness, courage, humility, and resilience. His eternal life serves as a metaphor for the timeless potential within each of us to transcend the limitations of our physical existence by living in alignment with higher principles. By following Hanuman's example, we too can achieve a form of immortality, not through endless life but through the lasting impact of our actions, values, and dedication to a righteous path.

Hanuman's story reminds us that true immortality lies not in escaping death but in living a life of meaning, purpose, and service to others. When we align ourselves with the eternal truths that

Hanuman represents, we too can transcend the boundaries of time, leaving a legacy that endures in the hearts and minds of future generations.

CHAPTER XIII

Hanuman and the Mind: Mastering Inner Challenges

Overcoming Inner Demons: A Guide to Strengthening the Mind and Heart

In the rich tapestry of Hindu mythology, Hanuman stands out not only as a divine hero and protector but also as a profound symbol of mental mastery and inner strength. His journey, marked by feats of extraordinary physical prowess and unyielding devotion, also offers deep insights into the nature of the mind and the inner challenges that every individual faces. Hanuman's ability to overcome obstacles is not just a reflection of his external strength but also of his mastery over his inner self. This chapter explores Hanuman's relationship with the mind, offering insights into how his story can guide us in mastering our own inner challenges and achieving mental resilience.

The Concept of the Mind in Hindu Philosophy

To understand Hanuman's mastery over inner challenges, it is crucial to first explore the concept of the mind as presented in Hindu philosophy. The mind, or *manas*, is considered a powerful entity that influences our thoughts, emotions, and actions. It is often depicted as a battleground where various forces—desires, fears, doubts—compete for dominance. The mind is both a tool for achieving great things and a source of inner turmoil when not properly controlled.

In the Bhagavad Gita, Lord Krishna describes the mind as both a friend and an enemy. When disciplined and controlled, it serves as a powerful ally, guiding one towards spiritual growth and self-realization. However, when undisciplined, it becomes a source of inner conflict and distraction. This dual nature of the mind underscores the importance of mastering it to achieve inner peace and personal success.

Hanuman's journey and actions offer a rich narrative on how to achieve this mastery. His feats are not merely physical but deeply intertwined with his mental strength, focus, and discipline. By examining Hanuman's story, we can gain valuable insights into how to manage our own mental challenges and cultivate a mindset that aligns with our highest goals.

Hanuman's Self-Realization and Inner Strength

One of the most significant aspects of Hanuman's character is his journey toward self-realization. Despite his divine nature and immense power, Hanuman often forgets his own abilities. This forgetfulness is symbolic of the human condition where individuals are often unaware of their full potential. Hanuman's story of rediscovering his strength is a powerful metaphor for overcoming self-doubt and realizing one's inner capabilities.

In the Ramayana, there are moments when Hanuman's courage and strength are obscured by his own doubts. For instance, when he is about to cross the ocean to reach Lanka, he initially hesitates, plagued by fear and uncertainty. However, once he remembers his divine nature and the blessings of Lord Rama, he taps into his full potential and accomplishes the seemingly impossible task. This moment of self-realization is crucial, as it illustrates that inner strength is often unlocked through self-awareness and faith.

For individuals struggling with self-doubt or insecurity, Hanuman's journey offers a profound lesson: recognizing and embracing one's true potential is key to overcoming inner obstacles. Just as Hanuman needed a reminder of his own power, people too can benefit from practices that help them connect with their inner strengths, such as meditation, self-reflection, and positive affirmations.

Overcoming Mental Obstacles: Hanuman's Triumph Over Fear and Doubt

Hanuman's life is filled with instances where he confronts and overcomes mental obstacles such as fear, doubt, and anxiety. These inner challenges are universal experiences that can hinder personal growth and achievement. Hanuman's responses to these challenges provide a template for how to navigate and master similar obstacles in our own lives.

The episode where Hanuman flies to Lanka to find Sita is particularly instructive. At the onset of this mission, Hanuman is confronted by the enormity of the task ahead. The vast ocean and the formidable city of Lanka are symbols of his fears and doubts. However, through his mental discipline and focus, he overcomes these challenges. Hanuman's ability to rise above his fears and doubts is rooted in his unwavering devotion to Lord Rama and his clear understanding of his purpose.

This aspect of Hanuman's character teaches us that overcoming mental obstacles requires a combination of focus, clarity of purpose, and inner strength. By cultivating these qualities, individuals can better manage their own fears and doubts. Practical strategies for achieving this include setting clear goals, practicing mindfulness, and engaging in self-discipline. Hanuman's triumph over his mental barriers serves as an inspiring example of how to confront and conquer internal struggles.

The Role of Devotion in Mental Mastery

Hanuman's story is deeply intertwined with his devotion to Lord Rama, and this devotion plays a crucial role in his ability to master his mind. Devotion, or *bhakti*, is more than just an external practice; it is a profound inner commitment that shapes one's thoughts, emotions, and actions. Hanuman's unwavering love and dedication to Lord Rama provide him with the mental strength and clarity needed to overcome challenges.

In Hindu philosophy, devotion is considered a powerful force that can transform the mind and spirit. When one is devoted to a higher purpose or divine being, it aligns the mind with positive, constructive energies. This alignment helps in overcoming negative mental states such as fear, anger, and confusion. Hanuman's example demonstrates that a strong sense of devotion can provide a steady foundation for mental resilience.

For individuals seeking to harness the power of devotion in their own lives, it is important to identify and connect with a purpose or cause that resonates deeply with them. This could be a personal goal, a spiritual practice, or a commitment to helping others. By dedicating oneself to a higher purpose, individuals can cultivate a sense of inner strength and focus that helps in mastering mental challenges.

Mindfulness and Presence: Hanuman's Focused Mind

Another key aspect of Hanuman's mastery over his mind is his ability to maintain mindfulness and presence. Throughout his adventures, Hanuman demonstrates exceptional focus and concentration, whether he is battling demons, carrying the mountain of herbs, or performing acts of heroism. His ability to stay fully engaged in the task at hand is a testament to his mental discipline.

In the Ramayana, Hanuman's acts of heroism are not only physical feats but also reflections of his mental focus and clarity. For example, when he leaps across the ocean to reach Lanka, his concentration on the mission and his unwavering belief in his capabilities are crucial to his success. This ability to remain present and focused amidst challenges is a valuable lesson for mastering the mind.

In modern life, mindfulness and presence can be cultivated through practices such as meditation, deep breathing, and conscious awareness. These practices help individuals stay grounded in the present moment, reducing the impact of stress, anxiety, and distractions. By incorporating mindfulness techniques into daily routines, individuals can enhance their mental clarity and effectiveness, much like Hanuman's focused approach in his endeavors.

Embracing Challenges as Opportunities for Growth

Hanuman's life is a series of challenges and obstacles that he embraces as opportunities for growth. His journey is a powerful reminder that challenges are not merely obstacles but can be transformative experiences that lead to greater self-discovery and development. Hanuman's ability to view challenges through this lens of growth is a key aspect of his mental mastery.

For example, Hanuman's mission to rescue Sita involves numerous trials and confrontations with powerful adversaries. Each challenge he faces is an opportunity for him to demonstrate his strength, courage, and devotion. By embracing these challenges and using them as opportunities to showcase his virtues, Hanuman reinforces the idea that adversity can lead to personal growth and enlightenment.

In our own lives, embracing challenges with a positive mindset can lead to significant personal development. Viewing obstacles as opportunities for growth allows individuals to approach difficulties with resilience and optimism. This perspective shift can transform how one handles life's trials, turning potential setbacks into valuable learning experiences.

The Integration of Mental and Physical Mastery

Hanuman's story also highlights the integration of mental and physical mastery. While his physical feats are well-known, they are deeply connected to his mental discipline. His ability to perform extraordinary physical acts is a direct result of his mental focus, determination, and clarity of purpose. This integration of mind and body is essential for achieving holistic mastery.

The concept of integrating mental and physical aspects is supported by various philosophical and psychological theories. The idea that mental strength enhances physical performance and vice versa is well-documented in modern psychology and wellness practices. Hanuman's life exemplifies this integration, demonstrating that achieving balance between mental clarity and physical capability can lead to extraordinary outcomes.

For individuals looking to cultivate this integration, it is important to engage in practices that strengthen both mind and body. This includes physical exercise, mental training, and activities that promote overall well-being. By nurturing both aspects, individuals can achieve a more balanced and effective approach to personal growth and success.

Hanuman's Role as a Mentor and Guide: Lessons for the Modern Mind

In addition to his heroic deeds, Hanuman is also depicted as a mentor and guide to other characters in the Ramayana. His wisdom, compassion, and understanding of the mind make him an invaluable advisor to those who seek his counsel. This role as a mentor highlights the importance of guiding others in mastering their own mental challenges.

Hanuman's interactions with other characters, such as Rama and Lakshmana, are marked by his deep understanding of their needs and his ability to provide guidance and support. His role as a mentor is not only a reflection of his divine nature but also a model for how individuals can help others navigate their own mental and emotional challenges.

For those seeking to emulate Hanuman's role as a guide, it is important to cultivate qualities such as empathy, patience, and wisdom. Offering support and guidance to others, whether through mentoring, counseling, or simply being a compassionate friend, can have a profound impact on their ability to master their own inner challenges. By embodying these qualities, individuals can contribute to the mental well-being and growth of those around them.

Conclusion: Mastering the Mind through Hanuman's Example

In conclusion, Hanuman's story offers profound insights into mastering the mind and overcoming inner challenges. His journey, marked by self-realization, mental discipline, and unwavering devotion, provides a powerful framework for understanding and managing the complexities of the human mind. Hanuman's ability to transcend fear, doubt, and adversity serves as a model for how individuals can cultivate mental resilience and clarity.

By embracing the lessons from Hanuman's life, individuals can learn to recognize and harness their inner strengths, overcome mental obstacles, and achieve a balanced and focused mindset. Hanuman's example demonstrates that mastering the mind is not just about overcoming internal struggles but also about aligning oneself with higher principles and purpose.

Through practices such as mindfulness, self-reflection, and devotion, individuals can achieve greater mental clarity and resilience, ultimately leading to personal growth and success. Hanuman's eternal relevance as a symbol of mental mastery and inner strength continues to inspire and guide those seeking to navigate their own inner challenges and achieve their fullest potential.

CHAPTER XIV

Embodying Hanuman's Values in Daily Life

Walking the Path of Devotion: Integrating Hanuman's Teachings in Everyday Living

Hanuman, the divine monkey warrior from Hindu mythology, is not only a figure of immense strength and devotion but also a beacon of values that can be meaningfully integrated into daily life. His character, with its profound virtues of devotion, humility, courage, and resilience, offers practical lessons that transcend cultural and religious boundaries. This chapter explores how one can embody Hanuman's values in everyday living, providing a detailed and practical guide to applying his timeless principles to personal and professional aspects of life. Through the examination of his core attributes and their application, readers will find inspiration and actionable insights to enhance their lives.

The Essence of Hanuman's Values

At the heart of Hanuman's legendary status are several key virtues that define his character and actions. His devotion to Lord Rama, his unparalleled strength, his humility despite immense power, and his resilience in the face of adversity form the cornerstone of his identity. Each of these values is not only central to Hanuman's story but also offers a blueprint for personal growth and ethical living.

Devotion, in Hanuman's case, is an unwavering commitment to a higher purpose or cause. This form of dedication goes beyond mere adherence to duties; it is about embodying a deep sense of purpose that guides one's actions and decisions. Hanuman's strength is both physical and mental, reflecting the power of discipline, focus, and the ability to overcome obstacles. Humility, despite his divine prowess, underscores the importance of staying grounded and recognizing the contributions of others. Finally, Hanuman's resilience showcases the power of perseverance and inner fortitude when faced with challenges.

Incorporating Devotion into Daily Life

The virtue of devotion, as exemplified by Hanuman, can be transformative when applied to daily life. It involves a deep-seated commitment to one's goals, relationships, and values, fostering a sense of purpose and direction.

To embody devotion in daily life, start by identifying your core values and goals. These might be related to personal development, professional aspirations, or commitments to family and community. Just as Hanuman's devotion to Lord Rama guided his every action, having a clear sense of purpose can provide motivation and clarity in your own life.

Establishing a routine that aligns with your values is crucial. This could involve setting aside time for activities that reinforce your goals, such as learning new skills, engaging in meaningful work, or spending quality time with loved ones. Consistency in these efforts mirrors Hanuman's dedication to his mission, showing that regular, purposeful actions lead to significant progress over time.

Moreover, true devotion also means being committed to the well-being of others. Hanuman's service to Lord Rama was driven by his desire to help and protect. Similarly, integrating acts of kindness and support into your daily routine can reflect this principle. Whether it's offering assistance to a colleague, being present for a friend in need, or volunteering for community service, these actions demonstrate a devotion to the welfare of others and contribute to a more compassionate world.

Strength and Discipline: Building Resilience

Hanuman's remarkable strength, both physical and mental, is a testament to his discipline and resilience. To embody this value in daily life, focus on developing both physical fitness and mental fortitude.

Physical strength can be cultivated through regular exercise and maintaining a healthy lifestyle. This includes engaging in activities that challenge your body, such as strength training, cardio exercises, or sports. Just as Hanuman's physical feats were supported by his disciplined training, personal fitness routines build strength and endurance, contributing to overall well-being and resilience.

Mental strength, on the other hand, involves cultivating focus, determination, and the ability to handle stress. Practices such as meditation, mindfulness, and setting clear, achievable goals can enhance mental discipline. Hanuman's ability to stay focused on his mission, even under extreme pressure, serves as an inspiration to develop a resilient mindset. Techniques such as visualization, positive affirmations, and stress management strategies can help in building mental toughness.

Resilience, an essential aspect of Hanuman's character, is about overcoming setbacks and persisting in the face of adversity. Embracing challenges as opportunities for growth rather than obstacles can transform your approach to difficulties. By viewing failures and setbacks as learning experiences, you can develop a resilient attitude that mirrors Hanuman's unwavering spirit.

Practicing Humility: Staying Grounded

Despite his divine nature and extraordinary abilities, Hanuman is celebrated for his humility. This quality is vital in maintaining balanced relationships and fostering personal growth.

To practice humility, start by acknowledging and appreciating the contributions of others in your life. Recognize that achievements are often the result of collective efforts and support. Expressing gratitude to those who assist you and giving credit where it is due reflects a humble attitude and strengthens interpersonal relationships.

Humility also involves being open to feedback and learning from others. Hanuman's humility allowed him to learn and grow continuously. Similarly, being receptive to constructive criticism and seeking opportunities for self-improvement can enhance personal and professional development.

In professional settings, humility can be demonstrated through collaborative teamwork, where the focus is on collective success rather than individual glory. Leading by example, being approachable, and showing respect for others' ideas and contributions foster a positive and productive work environment.

Resilience in the Face of Adversity

Hanuman's story is a testament to resilience—the ability to bounce back from adversity and continue pursuing one's goals despite obstacles. Incorporating resilience into daily life involves developing a mindset that embraces challenges and views them as opportunities for growth.

One way to build resilience is through setting realistic and achievable goals. Break larger tasks into smaller, manageable steps and celebrate progress along the way. This approach mirrors Hanuman's methodical efforts in overcoming challenges, ensuring that each small victory contributes to overall success.

Developing coping strategies for dealing with stress and setbacks is also crucial. Techniques such as deep breathing, journaling, and seeking support from others can help manage stress and maintain focus during difficult times. Hanuman's ability to maintain composure and determination in the face of formidable challenges serves as a model for managing adversity with grace and resilience.

Additionally, cultivating a growth mindset can enhance resilience. This mindset involves viewing challenges as opportunities to learn and improve rather than as threats to success. Embracing this perspective allows you to approach difficulties with a positive attitude and a willingness to adapt and grow, just as Hanuman did in his various missions.

Service and Compassion: Contributing to Others

Hanuman's unwavering service to Lord Rama and his compassion for others highlight the importance of contributing to the well-being of those around us. Incorporating service and compassion into daily life involves actively seeking opportunities to help and support others, whether through direct actions or through fostering a caring attitude.

Acts of service can range from volunteering for community organizations to simply offering a helping hand to a friend or colleague. Engaging in charitable activities, participating in community outreach programs, or supporting causes that align with your values are all ways to embody Hanuman's spirit of service.

Compassion involves more than just actions; it requires a genuine empathy and understanding towards others' experiences and needs. Practicing active listening, showing kindness, and offering support in times of need reflect a compassionate attitude. Hanuman's ability to empathize with Lord Rama's plight and his readiness to assist in any way possible exemplify the depth of compassion that can enhance interpersonal relationships and community well-being.

Balancing Action and Reflection: The Path to Personal Growth

Hanuman's actions, driven by purpose and commitment, are balanced by moments of reflection and strategic planning. This balance between action and reflection is crucial for personal growth and effective decision-making.

To achieve this balance, it is essential to allocate time for both proactive efforts and contemplative practices. Setting aside time for reflection, whether through meditation, journaling, or quiet contemplation, allows you to evaluate your actions, assess progress, and make informed decisions. Hanuman's strategic approach to his missions, combined with his active efforts, underscores the importance of both planning and execution.

Additionally, regular self-assessment and goal-setting can help align your actions with your values and objectives. Reflect on your experiences, learn from them, and adjust your strategies as needed. This reflective practice not only supports personal growth but also enhances the effectiveness of your efforts, ensuring that your actions remain purposeful and aligned with your long-term goals.

Incorporating Hanuman's Values into Professional Life

Hanuman's virtues can also be applied to professional settings, where his values of devotion, strength, humility, and resilience are equally relevant. In the workplace, embodying these values can lead to enhanced performance, better relationships with colleagues, and greater overall satisfaction.

Devotion to one's work involves a commitment to excellence and a dedication to achieving professional goals. Approaching tasks with a sense of purpose and enthusiasm, seeking opportunities for growth, and contributing to the success of your team reflect Hanuman's dedication to his mission.

Strength and discipline in the professional realm are demonstrated through perseverance, focus, and the ability to overcome challenges. Maintaining a strong work ethic, staying motivated despite setbacks, and continuously striving for improvement embody the strength and resilience that Hanuman exemplifies.

Humility in the workplace involves recognizing and valuing the contributions of others, being open to feedback, and fostering a collaborative environment. Acknowledging the role of teamwork and being receptive to different perspectives reflect a humble and inclusive approach.

Resilience is crucial for navigating the ups and downs of professional life. Developing strategies to manage stress, adapt to changes, and persist in the face of obstacles can enhance your ability to handle challenges effectively. Hanuman's resilience in his various adventures serves as a powerful model for maintaining composure and determination in the professional sphere.

Conclusion: Living Hanuman's Values Every Day

In conclusion, embodying Hanuman's values in daily life involves integrating his virtues of devotion, strength, humility, and resilience into every aspect of personal and professional living. His character serves as a timeless model for navigating life's challenges, fostering personal growth, and contributing positively to the well-being of others.

By embracing Hanuman's principles, individuals can cultivate a sense of purpose and direction, develop resilience and mental strength, and maintain humility and compassion in their interactions. These values not only enhance personal and professional effectiveness but also contribute to a more meaningful and fulfilling life.

As you apply Hanuman's values to your daily life, remember that his story is not just a historical or mythological account but a source of practical wisdom and inspiration. His example demonstrates that living with devotion, strength, humility, and resilience can lead to personal growth, positive impact, and a deeper connection to one's purpose and values. By embodying these virtues, you can navigate life's challenges with grace and determination, ultimately achieving a life of greater fulfillment and significance.

CHAPTER XV

Conclusion The Enduring Legacy of Lord Hanuman

Embracing the Eternal Teachings of the Divine Warrior

In the rich tapestry of Hindu mythology, few figures stand as tall, both literally and figuratively, as Lord Hanuman. From the moment of his miraculous birth to his exploits in the epic Ramayana, Hanuman's life is a testament to the power of devotion, strength, wisdom, and humility. But beyond the legendary feats and divine powers, Hanuman represents ideals that are universally relevant, transcending the bounds of time, culture, and religion. As we draw our exploration of Hanuman's life and teachings to a close, it becomes clear that his legacy is not just a relic of the past but a living force that continues to inspire and guide humanity in the modern world.

The Symbolism of Hanuman: A Bridge Between the Divine and the Human

Hanuman's life is a bridge between the mortal and the divine, the earthly and the spiritual. His character is a blend of divinity and humanity, showcasing qualities that are both superhuman and deeply relatable. This duality is what makes Hanuman such a compelling figure, both as a mythological character and as a symbol of spiritual ideals.

On one hand, Hanuman is a divine being with extraordinary powers—able to leap across oceans, carry mountains, and change his size at will. These abilities make him an awe-inspiring figure, revered by devotees for his strength and power. Yet, on the other hand, Hanuman is also profoundly human. He experiences emotions, faces challenges, and learns important lessons throughout his life. His deep devotion to Lord Rama, his humility despite his power, and his unwavering commitment to righteousness are qualities that resonate with the human experience. They remind us that even in our human limitations, we have the potential to embody divine qualities through our actions and choices.

This duality of Hanuman as both divine and human symbolizes the potential within each of us to transcend our limitations and connect with the divine. Hanuman's life encourages us to see the divine within ourselves and others, to recognize that our highest aspirations—whether they are for strength, wisdom, or devotion—are not beyond our reach. In this way, Hanuman serves as a bridge between the mortal world and the divine, reminding us of the interconnectedness of all life and the possibility of living a life that reflects our highest values.

Hanuman's Devotion: A Model for Spiritual Practice

At the heart of Hanuman's legacy is his unwavering devotion to Lord Rama, a devotion that goes beyond mere loyalty or duty. Hanuman's devotion is total, encompassing every aspect of his being—his thoughts, actions, and even his identity. He sees himself not as an independent entity but as a servant of Rama, finding his purpose and fulfillment in serving the divine will.

This level of devotion, known as *bhakti* in the Hindu tradition, is a powerful model for spiritual practice. Bhakti is not about ritualistic worship or blind faith; it is about cultivating a deep, personal relationship with the divine, one that transforms every aspect of one's life. Hanuman's bhakti is characterized by selflessness, humility, and surrender. He does not seek rewards or recognition for his service; his only desire is to fulfill Rama's mission and to be close to his beloved Lord.

In the modern world, where the pursuit of material success often takes precedence over spiritual growth, Hanuman's devotion offers a profound lesson. It reminds us that true fulfillment comes not from the accumulation of wealth or power, but from living in alignment with our highest principles and dedicating ourselves to a purpose greater than ourselves. Hanuman's life encourages us to cultivate a sense of devotion in our own lives, whether it is through a relationship with the divine, a commitment to a cause, or a dedication to serving others.

Moreover, Hanuman's devotion is a reminder of the transformative power of love. His love for Rama is not just emotional but spiritual, a love that transcends the physical and the material. This type of love, known as *prema* in the Hindu tradition, is a state of being that connects us to the divine and to each other. Hanuman's prema for Rama inspires us to cultivate a love that is selfless, unconditional, and eternal, a love that uplifts and transforms both the giver and the receiver.

The Power of Strength and Resilience in Overcoming Life's Challenges

Hanuman's physical strength is legendary, but it is his inner strength that truly defines him. Throughout the Ramayana, Hanuman faces numerous challenges—crossing the ocean to Lanka, confronting the powerful demon king Ravana, and undertaking the perilous mission to find the Sanjeevani herb to save Lakshmana. In each of these situations, Hanuman's strength is not just about his physical abilities but about his determination, courage, and resilience.

In the face of seemingly insurmountable obstacles, Hanuman remains steadfast and focused on his mission. He does not allow fear or doubt to deter him; instead, he draws upon his inner strength and faith in Rama to overcome every challenge. This resilience is a key aspect of Hanuman's character and a quality that is deeply relevant in today's world.

Modern life is filled with challenges—whether they are personal, professional, or social. The pressures of daily life, the uncertainty of the future, and the complexities of relationships can often feel overwhelming. Hanuman's example teaches us that we all have the strength within us to face these challenges. His life encourages us to cultivate resilience, to develop the mental and emotional strength to persevere in the face of adversity.

Moreover, Hanuman's strength is not about brute force; it is about the strength of character. It is about having the courage to stand up for what is right, even when it is difficult. It is about the determination to keep going, even when the path is uncertain. Hanuman's life reminds us that true strength is not just physical but also moral and spiritual, and that this strength can be developed through practice, discipline, and devotion.

The Wisdom of Hanuman: Discernment and Humility in Decision-Making

Hanuman is often celebrated for his physical feats, but his wisdom and discernment are equally important aspects of his character. Throughout the Ramayana, Hanuman demonstrates a deep understanding of dharma, the moral and ethical principles that govern the universe. His decisions are always guided by a sense of righteousness and justice, and he has the ability to see through deception and recognize the truth in any situation.

One of the most striking examples of Hanuman's wisdom is his encounter with Sita in Lanka. After finding Sita in Ravana's Garden, Hanuman could have easily attacked the demon guards and rescued her immediately. However, he recognizes that this is not the right course of action. Instead, he carefully considers the situation and decides to first reassure Sita of Rama's love and commitment, and then return to Rama with news of her location. This decision reflects Hanuman's ability to think strategically, to understand the long-term consequences of his actions, and to prioritize the greater good over immediate gratification.

In the modern world, where quick decisions and instant results are often valued, Hanuman's wisdom offers a powerful lesson in the importance of discernment and patience. His example encourages us to take the time to carefully consider our actions, to think about their impact on others, and to make decisions that are in alignment with our values and principles.

Furthermore, Hanuman's wisdom is deeply connected to his humility. Despite his extraordinary abilities, Hanuman never allows pride or ego to cloud his judgment. He is always willing to learn, to seek advice, and to act in the best interests of others. This humility is a key aspect of true wisdom, as it allows us to remain open to new perspectives and to make decisions based on what is right, rather than what will enhance our own status or power.

In a world where ego and self-interest often drive decision-making, Hanuman's humility offers a different model of leadership and wisdom. His life teaches us that true wisdom is grounded in selflessness, in the willingness to serve others and to act with integrity, even when it is difficult. Hanuman's example reminds us that the wisest decisions are those that are made with a clear mind and a pure heart, with the well-being of others in mind.

Hanuman's Humility: The Foundation of True Greatness

One of the most remarkable aspects of Hanuman's character is his humility. Despite his immense power and the pivotal role, he plays in the Ramayana, Hanuman never seeks personal glory or recognition. He always attributes his successes to the grace of Lord Rama and sees himself as merely an instrument of Rama's will. This humility is not just a personal trait but a reflection of Hanuman's deep spiritual understanding.

Hanuman's humility is rooted in his recognition of the divine within all beings. He does not see himself as separate from others or as superior because of his abilities. Instead, he sees himself as part of the greater whole, as a servant of the divine. This perspective allows him to act with compassion, kindness, and respect towards everyone he encounters, regardless of their status or abilities.

In the modern world, where success is often measured by personal achievements and accolades, Hanuman's humility offers a powerful counter-narrative. His life reminds us that true greatness is not about what we achieve for ourselves but about how we serve others. Hanuman's humility teaches us that the most enduring form of greatness is that which is grounded in selflessness, in the willingness to put the needs of others before our own, and in the recognition that our true purpose lies in serving the greater good.

Moreover, Hanuman's humility is a reminder of the importance of gratitude. Throughout his life, Hanuman remains deeply grateful for the opportunities he has to serve Rama and for the grace that allows him to accomplish his tasks. This gratitude is a key aspect of his humility, as it keeps him grounded and prevents him from becoming arrogant or complacent.

In today's world, where entitlement and self-centeredness are often prevalent, Hanuman's example of humility and gratitude offers a powerful lesson. His life encourages us to cultivate a sense of humility in our own lives, to recognize that our abilities and achievements are gifts that come with the responsibility to use them for the benefit of others. Hanuman's humility reminds us that the most important thing is not what we achieve but how we live, and that true greatness lies in living with humility, gratitude, and a commitment to serving the greater good.

Hanuman's Legacy: A Timeless Guide for Modern Life

As we reflect on the life and teachings of Hanuman, it becomes clear that his legacy is not just a story from the past but a timeless guide for modern life. Hanuman's devotion, strength, wisdom, and humility offer valuable lessons for navigating the challenges and opportunities of contemporary life. His example teaches us that true success and fulfillment come not from selfish pursuits but from living a life of purpose, integrity, and service to others.

In a world that is often characterized by materialism, competition, and division, Hanuman's legacy serves as a powerful reminder of the importance of spiritual values such as love, compassion, and humility. His life shows us that these values are not just abstract ideals but practical qualities that can guide our actions and decisions in everyday life. By embodying these qualities, we can find the strength and wisdom to face the challenges of the modern world and to live lives that are meaningful, fulfilling, and aligned with our highest aspirations.

Furthermore, Hanuman's influence in the modern world is a reflection of the enduring power of myth and symbolism in human life. His stories continue to inspire and uplift people across cultures and generations, offering a source of hope and guidance in times of difficulty. Whether we encounter Hanuman in a temple, in a work of art, or in the stories passed down through generations, his presence reminds us of the eternal truths that underlie our existence and the potential we all have to rise above our limitations and achieve greatness.

Hanuman's legacy is also a reminder of the power of faith and devotion in our lives. His unwavering commitment to Rama, his trust in the divine plan, and his willingness to surrender his own desires in service to the greater good are qualities that can inspire us to deepen our own spiritual practice. Hanuman's life teaches us that faith is not just about belief but about action—about living in a way that reflects our deepest values and our trust in the divine.

In conclusion, Hanuman's legacy is a beacon of light in the modern world, offering timeless lessons for all who seek to live with purpose, integrity, and spiritual depth. His life is a testament to the power of devotion, strength, wisdom, and humility, and his teachings continue to inspire and guide us on our journey through life. By following Hanuman's example, we can find the inspiration and guidance needed to navigate the complexities of modern life and to live in a way that is true to our highest ideals. Hanuman's legacy continues to shine as a source of hope, wisdom, and inspiration for all who seek to live a life of meaning and purpose in the modern world.

Author's Note

Dear reader,
Thank you for embarking on this spiritual journey with me. I hope this book has brought you closer to understanding the profound lessons Lord Hanuman has to offer. May his virtues guide you toward strength, humility, and devotion in your own life.

.

About The Author

Mukesh Bharti is a testament to perseverance and the relentless pursuit of excellence. His journey through life is marked by a series of remarkable transformations, rising from humble beginnings to achieve significant milestones in his professional career. Mukesh's story is one of resilience, adaptability, and a deep commitment to personal growth.

Born into a world of challenges, Mukesh Bharti started his career with labor-intensive work, a path that taught him the values of hard work, determination, and the importance of seizing opportunities, no matter how small. These early experiences laid a solid foundation for his character, instilling in him a unique perspective on life and work.

As Mukesh navigated through life's ups and downs, he never lost sight of his ambitions. His unwavering dedication and continuous learning enabled him to climb the professional ladder.

Mukesh Bharti's life is a source of inspiration for those who face adversities and aspire to rise above them. His journey is a powerful reminder that no matter where one starts, with the right mindset and perseverance, the possibilities are endless.

Enter Caption